KnitLit

D1019022

KnitLit

Sweaters and Their Stories . . . and Other Writing About Knitting

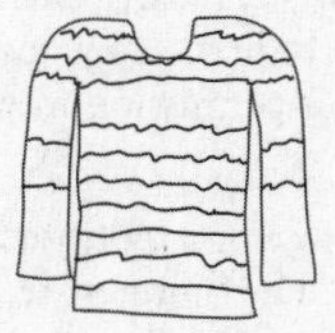

Linda Roghaar &
Molly Wolf, editors

THREE RIVERS PRESS
NEW YORK

"Twenty Years and Still Growing" reprinted by permission from *Interweave Knits,* Fall 2001. "The Spinner" reprinted from *Hiding in Plain Sight: Sabbath Blessings,* by permission of The Liturgical Press.

Published by Three Rivers Press, New York, New York. Member of the Crown Publishing Group, a division of Random House, Inc.

www.randomhouse.com

Printed in the United States of America

DESIGN BY ELINA D. NUDELMAN

Library of Congress Cataloging-in-Publication Data
KnitLit : sweaters and their stories . . . and other writing about knitting / Linda Roghaar and Molly Wolf, editors.
1. Knitting. 2. Knitting—Miscellanea. 3. Knitters (Persons)—Miscellanea. 4. Sweaters. I. Roghaar, Linda. II. Wolf, Molly.
TT825 .K639 2002
746.43'2—dc21 2002005962

ISBN 0-609-80824-9

10 9 8 7 6 5

First Edition

Contents

Bodacious Knits

Extreme Knitting

PART TWO: *Fleece, Fur, and Foreign Lands*

Yarns and Needles

Mercies for the Children (and the Earth)

All Creatures Great and Small

Peaceable Fleece in Foreign Parts

PART THREE: *Family and Special Folk*

Grandmothers

The Reluctant Child

Aunts and Other Friends

The Guys in Our Lives

PART FOUR: *Lives and Souls*

Lives

Foreword

Melanie Falick

Aside from a soft click-clack from the needles, knitting is mostly a silent medium. Though knitters can work and converse, there is rarely a need for words spoken aloud. Knitters use their fingers, their needles, and their yarn to create stitches that hold within them their thoughts and wishes. A pregnant woman knits for her soon-to-be-born baby. With her stitches she says, "I want to keep you safe, I want to keep you warm, I love you." A mother knits a sweater for her grown child who lives far away. Into the stitches, she knits the same message, with maybe a "Please call me" added on. A wife sits in a hospital waiting for her husband to come through surgery and knits to calm herself, to give herself something to do with her hands while she begs invisible powers to heal her beloved.

To people who have never knitted or never received a handknit from someone significant to them, this may seem strange. To knitters, recipients of handknits, and the writers who contributed the essays in *KnitLit*, I am sure this concept of silent, intimate communication through knitting makes perfect sense.

In "Peace Fleece," Peter Hagerty writes about how during the throes of the Cold War he came up with the idea of combining wool from Russia with wool from the United States to create a yarn that would say, "At our core, we are more the same than we are different. Peace." In "A Twist in the Yarn," Zoë Blacksin recalls her grandmother telling her how her mother would "whisper prayers" into her wool. In "The Baby Blanket," Jean Stone writes about knitting a blanket for the baby she gave up for adoption; within the stitches were her prayers for his good life. In knitting, all of these people have found a voice, a way of expressing both who they are and what they feel. They have found a way of touching their core—their soul—and letting others around them touch it as well.

In this book, knitters—and people whose lives have been touched by knitting—tell their stories. Some are happy; some are sad. They take place in homes, on mountains, on the road, and amidst travel to faraway lands. Though they are all different, in one way or another, they all deliver a similar message: Knitting may not, on the surface, seem relevant to the engines that run the world, but at its essence, it is actually quite vital. For knitting, which can express so many emotions, most often expresses love. And when all else is lost, love is what most often stays with us.

Melanie Falick is editor-in-chief of *Interweave Knits* magazine, coauthor of *Knitting for Baby* (Stewart, Tabori & Chang, 2002), and author of *Kids Knitting* (Artisan, 1998) and *Knitting in America* (Artisan, 1995).

Preface: A Conversation

Molly says:

Since it was Linda's idea in the first place, she should go first.

Linda says:

I want to share with you a memory that I haven't thought of for years, until I started to write this introduction. . . . When I was in elementary school, every fall my mother made the most wonderful knee socks for me. They had cables, ribs, and patterns, and they matched my outfits perfectly. She also made special garters to hold them up. For all those years, I wore skirts every day, but my feet and legs were never cold.

I learned to knit as a child. But I didn't discover the connection between knitting and love until I began to knit sweaters for my high school boyfriend. I carefully threaded my blond hair into each oversized, misshapen sweater, and he wore them—wore them faithfully, and in public. My mother would look at him wearing one of those monstrosities, and she would shake her head and say, "That boy really loves you!" When he and I parted, I stopped knitting. I didn't pick up the needles again for thirty years.

At a camp reunion a few years ago, I reconnected with my childhood friends. By now they were (almost) all knitting, joyously obsessed with luscious yarns. I said, "I used to know how to knit," and my friend Janet told me, "Your hands remember." She was right. I went home from the reunion and straight to my local yarn shop. My hands *did* remember, and soon I too was hooked. (Is obsessed too strong a word?)

I found that knitting books were lovely, useful, and full of patterns and history. But one of the things I loved most about knitting was the stories knitters share with each other as they work, and I found no books of those stories. So much of my own work these days revolves around community and the strength and support I receive from it. I realized that the knitting community, which overlaps so many others, is about connection and love. I wanted a book about that connection. And that's how the idea for *KnitLit* came to be.

Now, I have done much of the "end work" of publishing—through my career in book sales and marketing and as a literary agent. But I had never in my life actually made a book. I knew I needed help. I called my friend and colleague Molly Wolf, who, as an author, editor, and indexer, has done all the other parts of bookmaking from soup to nuts. The two of us split the responsibility for the project: I solicited contributions, connected with our publisher, Three Rivers Press, and organized the promotion and publicity. Molly, who has a gift for organizing literary shoeboxes, sorted through the contributions, picked out those that fit with our theme of community and story-telling, and gave each piece a light editorial going-over.

Molly says:

As I went through the stack of contributions that Linda had put together, I found something curious and wonderful. All the stories had, of course, something to do with knitting, or with wool, or with sheep, or with dyeing—some sort of connection with those luscious yarns Linda's friends so loved and with the knitted stuff that people had made of them. But the best stories went much further than that. They were about wonder and suffering, love and high mountain paths, childhood and dancing with a dying grandmother. They were by turns poignant, funny, insightful, wise, strong-minded, deep, ebullient, and occasionally joyfully silly. Best of all, a fair number of them (and some of the best of them) came from men, not women. That was an unexpected pleasure.

I've found in my own writing that the best insights happen when you're most fully grounded in the here-and-now—when you're communing with the everyday and the practical. That's good woman-type wisdom. And that's what makes these stories work: that grounding. The yarn twists and turns, looping around, connecting souls, knitting community across boundaries in space and time—even across gaps in language. In that stack of written pieces, I did indeed find the community that Linda talks about. It makes for a lovely book.

Linda says:

This book is for my mother, Florence, and my daughters, Sarah and Hannah, knitters all. Thanks to Janet Blowney and all the other Hillsboro Campers who got me knitting again. See you on the Mess Hall porch! Thanks to Ellie for always being there, and to Jay.

This has been a collaborative effort from the beginning, and the book would not be what it is without invaluable help from Keri Anestis, Kristen Bahman, Kori Binette, Tara Cibelli, Erin Hamilton, Rachel Klein, Courtney Nolan, and Sian Wu. Thank you all for your help. To everyone who sent us a story, we thank you for sharing your experiences with us. We thank Becky Cabaza and Carrie Thornton of Three Rivers Press, who shared (and refined) our vision for the book.

Molly says:

Thanks, Linda. It's been a treat.

Linda Roghaar and Molly Wolf
Easter 2002

To our readers:

Have you got a knitting story you'd like to share? Something about sheep, or fleece, or anything else "from sheep to shawl"? We're already thinking about *KnitLit 2*. Contributions should be two or three pages long.

If you want more information, contact:

Linda Roghaar
PO Box 3561
Amherst, MA 01004-3561

or visit our website: www.knitlit.com

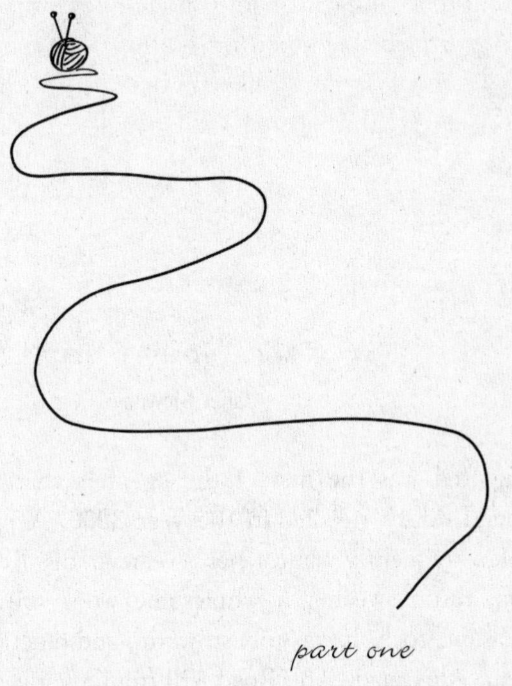

part one

projects

Names

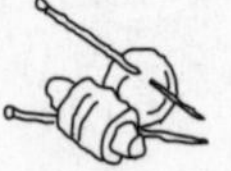

What's Your Name?

Janet Blowney

Big Red was the first of the sweaters that flew from my friend Alex's needles in the year 2000. A prolific knitter, Alex frequently names her sweaters. Big Red was a simple, rustic sweater, a wholesome wool sweater of hearty peasant stock. It was robust, warm, and practical. Later that year, Alex made The Road Kill from a variegated yarn purchased in an unguarded moment at the fabric store. The fleshy pinks and bilious greens created frightening patterns in the finished work. Looking at the sweater was like driving by the site of a terrible accident. Passersby paused despite themselves and shuddered, their eyes drawn to the violent acrylic splashes and swirls by some primal urge they did not understand. The Road Kill was one powerful sweater.

My projects, on the other hand, were unnamed, and often unfinished. Occasionally, if I stuck with a project long enough, I accepted a title offered by the pattern designer or the yarn maker. I finished the Artisan's Vest and the Putney Crofter without incident. I worked happily on the Mostly Merino sweater and the Great Adirondack scarf. Other projects, knit from less appealing yarns or more difficult patterns, languished, unnamed, on my needles. But sweater after sweater dropped from Alex's needles that year, as my pile of unfinished projects grew. I marveled at her productivity, at the number, variety, and complexity of her works. And I laughed at the creativity of their names. The naming was a natural part of the process. All of Alex's sweaters, it seemed, were named.

Then came the tunic known fondly as Brownie. The design and yarn were handpicked by a close friend, who delighted in the muted color, plain pattern, and enormous size of the garment. The friend loved the color; Alex found it drab. Still, Brownie was a birthday gift, and Alex cast on gamely. As the sweater progressed, her shoulders began to ache from flipping the full weight of the sweater on its huge circular needle. Alex was no longer fond of Brownie. The coarsely spun wool contained so much chaff that it wore holes in her hands. The project started as mindless, evolved to tedious, and fetched up as sheer drudgery. Before the last seam was sewn, Brownie had become The Beast, and I had glimpsed the real power of naming. This naming was more than just descriptive, I thought. It marked the transition that occurs in most knitting projects, when the knitter takes the precipitous step from the shining promise of the venture—all those lush colors, the intriguing pattern, the rich textures—and tumbles into the tedium, frustration, and reality of the undertaking. For the really tough projects, Alex's names were seldom affectionate.

"Name it, tame it," I mused. Perhaps to vanquish my own knitting furies I had to face them and name them. It was a grand thought, but my projects still remained unnamed and unfinished. A typical case was the baby sweater from That Certain Company. When I purchased the kit at the yarn store, it contained a cheerful designer yarn. The enclosed pattern showed an adorable sweater, just the thing for the upcoming baby shower. The package provided no inkling of the treachery within. I cast on innocently. At once, I was attacked by the eyelash yarn, which tangled fiercely. The colors clashed. The pattern refused to reveal its secrets. Throughout the ordeal, stitches vanished mysteriously from my needles and reappeared spontaneously days later at another location. Finally, I threw the sweater down in disgust: unnamed, unfinished. The date for the baby shower approached. I resumed my knitting, but without much hope of success. The yarn continued to put up a good fight. Snarls of eyelash peered up at me from the floor. I tugged and pulled, and the tangle grew, looking more and more like something regurgitated by the family pet. I gritted my teeth and gave a mighty yank. "Hair Ball," I hollered in frustration, and the tangle broke free. The rest of the knitting went without incident. The stitches marched in an orderly parade, in accordance with the printed instructions. The colors formed an alliance. Only days later at the shower, I proudly presented the expectant mother with the completed Hair Ball, wrapped carefully in pastel tissue paper. I'm confident the baby will look wonderful in it. (And no, I didn't let on what I'd named the thing.)

I've just cast on for another project. It's an intricately patterned pullover in a luxuriously soft, gray-green alpaca yarn. I have high hopes for its successful completion. Can anyone suggest a name?

Knitting Nancy

Nancy Chamberlin

Every story has a beginning and mine begins in my early teens. I was taught to knit by a left-handed friend. Since I am right-handed, my knitting ability and form are not the greatest. Nonetheless, over the years, I found knitting to be a great tool for relaxation purposes—until I became an alcoholic. Knitting then became a chore. There were too many dropped stitches and the patterns were too difficult to follow. After many years, I stopped fighting alcohol and started to attend meetings to learn how to live without drinking. I found it hard to focus on what the others said about learning to live in a sober reality. At this point, I started to knit again and I found it easier to concentrate when I was knitting. Thus knitting helped me to "learn to listen so I could listen to learn." Since people attending these meetings seldom if ever use last names, they often use adjectives to denote a particular person—Bald Harry or Mary with the Glasses, or the like. That's how I became known as Knitting Nancy. I'm happy to report that I still have the nickname over 31 years later.

Big Ugly

Rosalia Feinstein

One winter about thirty years ago, when I was at home with small children, I knitted two bulky cardigans for myself. In those years, I never re-knit anything. If it didn't fit right, I put it away or gave it away, but I never undid it and re-knit it to size. The first sweater (with matching hat) I knit with heathery gray bulky yarn. I made it big enough to wrap comfortably across my body. The cardigan ended up looking like a hip-length bathrobe, but I wore it for many years to work in the yard or to slip over my real bathrobe when running out to get the newspaper on chilly mornings. My second project that winter was a cardigan jacket. I still have the pattern for this item. The cover describes it as a wrapped cardigan, but the illustration shows several inches of space between the front panels, even on the model's skinny figure. Moreover, it was in early 1970s trendy orange. I knit it anyway. It was a disaster from the beginning. Even with my pattern adjustments, the sweater left a good twelve to fifteen inches of my ample bosom and belly exposed. Needless to say, I never wore it.

Some years later I went back to work. I loved my job and

my co-workers, but I hated the thermostat wars. You know—this woman's always too warm and the other one's always too cold. I was the lucky one. Management kept the place cool and I loved it that way. My secretary, Robin, was always chilly. She kept saying that she would be more comfortable with a blanket or something over her legs. Then I thought of that disastrous orange sweater. It was big enough and warm enough to be a lap blanket. I brought it in. Everyone who saw the sweater laughed. Here was this monstrously long sweater, knit to fit a size 3X body, in bright orange yarn. It was immediately christened Big Ugly. At first Robin used it like an afghan. Then, one day, she actually put it on and wore it around the office. That happened more and more often. One day, when Robin was absent, a co-worker came by to see if she could borrow Big Ugly that day. This began to happen with some frequency. People actually *wore* the thing, instead of draping it across their laps.

Big Ugly was an equal opportunity cardigan. It looked equally awful on tall people, short people, thin people, fat people, white people and people of color. I suspect it would have been just as ugly on a man if one of them had ever borrowed it. It was an act of courage to actually walk around wearing that thing, but it had the great advantage of being very warm and cozy. Periodically I would take Big Ugly home and wash it. Whatever I did, the orange synthetic yarn never faded, stretched or shrunk. It just stayed ugly.

When I retired after sixteen years in that office, I bequeathed Big Ugly to my co-workers. That was more than five years ago, before we moved to New Mexico. A few months ago we came back to Maryland for a wedding and I paid a visit to my old office. Guess what! The staff told me that Big Ugly was still around, still being actively worn by a variety of people. I have the feeling that Big Ugly will outlast all the people I worked with—that it's now a permanent office fixture. I hope its story lasts as long as Big Ugly itself.

Disasters

Burn Test

Jennifer Parko

"Excuse me, Miss. I think you're on fire."

Yes, yes I am and thanks for noticing. I am feeling particularly attractive tonight, and for a moment I'm thrilled that someone has noticed. It's odd, though, that everyone seems to notice. I'm not the sort of girl who turns heads when she enters a room. Someone at a nearby table points. In the foyer of one of the nicer bars in San Francisco, with low lights and lower necklines, almost everyone is looking at me. I'm not the sort of girl who turns heads in a place like this. Unless, of course, I'm actually *on fire*.

"Excuse me, Miss. You really are on fire."

This is not quite the case. First, I am not on fire, but my

knitting bag is. Second, it's not a flame, more like a slow smolder. If the gentleman had said correctly, "Excuse me, Miss. Your bag is smoldering," I could have stayed calm. Instead, I let out an appropriate shriek, ensuring that I've got the attention of everyone in the bar who is not already staring.

The contents of my knitting bag spill out onto the bar floor, and my first thought is, "Oh, no, now my sweater is going to get *dirty*!" At this moment, it doesn't seem to matter that it's burning so much as that it's touching a sticky bar floor. Instructions turn to ashes and the acrid smell of burning wool fills the bar. "This is what England smells like because of Hoof-and-Mouth Disease," I think to myself, as I begin patting out the smolder with my hands. A polite bystander tries to stomp on it, and I push the foot away. "This is my sweater," I think. You don't stomp on weeks of work, you gently pat. And then above me comes a cascade of water and ice. The man who was kind enough to tell me I'm on fire, puts me out.

A wet heap on the floor: twisted wool, a tape measure that has melted and welded itself to the circular needles, instructions that have turned to soot, and ice cubes with a twist of lime. And amidst it all, the culprit: the butt of a cigarette that someone has tossed into my open bag. The cigarette is burned down to cotton. I wonder just how long I was on fire. How far did I walk with a trail of smoke billowing behind me? Was the cigarette malicious, accidental, or strangely benevolent? Today is my 39th day without a cigarette and this cruel joke, this temptation, is not amusing.

"Excuse me, Miss. You can't smoke in here," the bartender says as he passes by. "I'm not smoking. I'm on fire. There's a difference." It's all become too ridiculous. I used to light cigarettes when I felt uncomfortable in public. That crutch is gone now, so I simply cry, "Could you please bring me a gin and tonic. I already have the lime."

I'm terrified to touch my sweater. I'm not ready to see how much of it has been lost. It's like the scene in a horror movie, when you know the bloody body lying facedown is dead, but the detective has to roll it over just so we can see the gory wounds. I hold the sweater up, the neck still bound to the holder. I look at the man who put me out, "I just finished the front. See. This is where I will start the neck. I wanted to finish it this weekend." I turn to the couple sitting next to him, to anyone who will listen. I look for the sympathetic face of a crafter, and all I get is bewilderment.

Crafters are hard to come by, knitters even more so. On the floor of this trendy bar I am alone. Knitters meet at homes and church basements, not in bars. That's a shame because knitting and bars seemed such a natural fit to me. Four years ago I thought, "If I want to quit smoking I need to do something with my hands." At bars, when others would light up I would pull out my knitting. K2P2 repeat. Bars are where I perfected much of my knitting. I did my first SSK in a small bar in Maine, and that simple act caused me to stand on my stool and proclaim, "I am a knitter!" I did my first cables while watching football in the Mission. But I was weak, and later in those bars I learned to master knitting with a cigarette dangling from my mouth, proving that I needed to do more than keep my hands busy to quit smoking. Later I tried gum and meditation, and then, a year ago I tried a patch. Everyone claimed the patch was the answer to my problem. But for the last 39 days it was determination that kept me from smoking. Determination, I learned, comes from knitting. I learned it staying up all night finishing a sweater on Christmas Eve; finishing a newborn-sized sweater for a child who had outgrown it months ago. Knitting gave me more than something to do with my hands.

In the restroom, at the counter a woman is reapplying makeup while I assess the damage. She smells like Chanel, I smell like Hoof-and-Mouth. "Honey, we thought you were so cool when you walked in. We thought you had dry ice in your bag." She fingers the border of the sweater, "This doesn't look bad. It's not a hole." And in her little world, she is right. The yarn still holds, but the sweet-pea green has turned to taupe in two large blots at the arm decrease. It looks like large coffee stains. I fantasize that I can pull it out, fix that section, and darn it together, but the truth is, I'll have to start over. I'll have to be determined and do it again. "Honey," she says with sympathy, "can't you just cut around it and put a patch on it?"

A patch. A *patch.* Thanks, lady. What a brilliant suggestion.

Road Kill

Lauren M. Baldwin

It's a sad, ratty-looking piece of knitting with large grease marks, dirt smudges and what look like large holes left by very satisfied moths. It was not always like this. It started out as a very respectable back of a brick-red Guernsey sweater that I was knitting from Debbie Bliss's *Classic Knits for Kids* in a double-knit washable wool. It was meant for a friend's son. As

I knit the bands of moss and garter stitch patterns across the chest, I savored the image of his dark eyes, fair skin and shock of dark brown hair against the brick-red wool.

Then came that Sunday after meeting (the Quaker term for "church") in early spring. I'd brought the red Guernsey project in my knitting bag, a large canvas contraption big enough to hide several half-finished projects, which I rationalize as artistic works in progress. After meeting, I carried the bag and my two-year-old son out to the car, set the bag down on the ground somewhere near the trunk and began the car-seat process with which so many of us are familiar. First, the child has to help unlock the car. Then comes the discussion about getting into the car and into the seat. He is firm in stating that he is very big now and can climb in by himself; that is, if he can find (after much searching) just the right handholds and footholds. Then, before he can sit down in his seat, he needs to show me how he can roll down the window by himself, and why, he asks, can he not have the window ALL the way down on the way home, because, "I will just be too hot, Mama, if not all down." At long last he was in and strapped and I got behind the wheel and backed up, presumably thinking about the next task in the day with a two-year-old.

Everything that happened next felt something like slow motion. As I drove through the parking lot, I noticed out of the corner of my eye what looked like a red string trailing behind the car. As my knitting bag slowly entered my consciousness as the possible source of the string and I began to realize I had left the bag behind the car, a woman in the parking lot started calling to me, yelling frantically that something was dragging under my car. Now fully comprehending what was happening, I screeched to a halt. Then I tried to nonchalantly run behind the car. There was the knitting bag, under the back end with the escaped ball of yarn trailing from the bag's gaping fish-mouth-like opening. Inside the bag was—not the back, but the partially completed front of the brick-red sweater dotted with grease and dirt smudges and a couple of skid marks—groups of two or three stitches which were just barely frayed. The completed back of the sweater was no longer in the bag but plastered up against my Mazda's undercarriage. I peeled it off and found myself staring at something that looked like a rag that the dog snuck into the backyard, chewed on and dragged through the dirt. It was definitely a casualty.

At this point I quickly began winding up the escaped ball of yarn through the parking lot. The woman who had sighted my knitting was eyeing me curiously, so I tried to act as though I pulled knitting from the undercarriage of my car and chased balls of yarn across parking lots every day. Meanwhile, I desperately wished I was a character in a sitcom making a perfect comedic exit: "Oh that! That's just my knitting. The car just backed over it. Excuse me, I'll just be going now."

In the car, I inspected the back of the sweater more closely. As I took in the grease marks, the dirt smudge that looked like a large boot print and those gaping holes, I started to cry. All that work—gone. It wasn't the most difficult sweater I'd ever knitted. It was not a deeply intricate or complicated design. It was not delicate or exotic wool on which I'd spent an entire paycheck. But it wasn't just work. It was my *knitting*.

In grappling with this loss, I found myself reflecting on creativity: how the things we make come to have emotional value. Partly we're attached to what we've made simply because we made it; but also, in the creative process we enter into a relationship with the thing we're working on. It comes to express something of ourselves. If the object is lost or destroyed, that bit of self is lost rather than captured and contained in the piece of creative work. And that is sad.

With time, I found some humor in this incident and I stopped chastising myself for my mistake. In fact, I began to wear the incident as something of a badge of honor. A few days after the disaster, I went to Village Wools here in Albuquerque and announced that I had the best knitting tragedy they had ever heard. I whipped out the sorry-looking back of the sweater and carefully explained that the car had backed over my knitting. Having placed blame properly on the car and avoided all form of personal responsibility, I went on to describe with great relish the knitting bag dragging on the ground beneath my car and the back of the sweater plastered to the undercarriage. The women at Village Wools laughed with me, but they also kindly and painstakingly examined the pieces of the sweater. We determined that the partially completed front was salvageable but the back was not. I washed the front and it was good as new. I reknit the back and the finished sweater was a great success at the little boy's birthday party in May that year.

The women at Village Wools told me I shouldn't throw away the damaged back of the sweater because it was such a priceless disaster piece. I promised them that one of these days I will frame it for them to hang in the store. But for now, I keep the piece around, tucked in a bag in my knitting basket—another large receptacle for hiding unfinished projects—perhaps because I'm still not quite ready to part with that bit of myself my fingers knitted into the wool. Or perhaps because, while it is a disaster which resulted from my own absentmindedness, it's *my* disaster and I'm not quite ready to give up on the imperfect piece of myself I keep in there.

Never Knit Dog

Anne McKee

My girlfriend Knits. I, for whom the term "opposable thumbs" is literal, sit and watch in amazement as she simultaneously knits, smokes, drinks rum and Diet Pepsi and shares choice bits of gossip from the small town in which we both live. She started, as I did, by knitting a scarf. Her first scarf was a work of art, lovingly labored over in those hours between her children's bedtime and her husband's return from working the evening shift. I, on the other hand, knit my scarf for my Barbie when I was ten, at the instigation of my mother, who felt I was not using my summer vacation time "wisely." I grudged every stitch. The scarf was, by mistake of measurement, twice the length of my Barbie and made out of some kind of synthetic material, dyed hot pink. It now takes up space in a landfill somewhere. It will never decompose.

I remember when my girlfriend took up knitting; cash was short and the Christmas season was looming. Sometime in the summer, a cloth bag full of wool and needles had been left at the playgroup we both attended, and never claimed. She snaffled it and proceeded to teach herself to knit. By my calculation this took a week of time, an extra half-pack of cigarettes and the kind of language that was rarely heard in the parsonage in which I was reared.

A week into the intense knitting campaign, when she'd taught herself to knit and smoke, but not knit, drink and smoke, she noticed that her chest was sore. It appeared that knitting was having an effect on her chest muscles. Her bra seemed tighter. Three weeks into the knitting campaign, by which time she could knit, drink, smoke and carry on a conversation, she noticed that her breasts appeared higher. Working those muscles was having a spectacular effect. This was good, I was told, very good. The knitting intensified. Her husband received the scarf on Christmas morning. When I called to inquire about its reception, I received the sort of information that falls into the category of "I-don't-want-to-know-I-don't-need-to-know-I-can't-ever-look-him-in-the-eye-again." He liked the scarf, but he *loved* the effect on her chest. Her career as a knitter achieved liftoff.

Her family began to expect knitted gifts for every occasion. It wasn't long before their wardrobes would put a Scottish closet to shame. She would lecture anyone who cared to listen (or anyone trapped with her in the checkout line of the local supermarket) on the varieties of wool, their color, texture, price. She began to crab about the price of wool at the local shops. She was sure there must be a cheaper way of getting wool.

And of course there was.

My girlfriend owned an Old English sheepdog, a large, hairy dog named Ben who shed copiously. The most fastidious housekeeper in the world could never have kept up with the hair produced by that dog. It was while cleaning one afternoon that my girlfriend was inspired with the notion that Ben's white and gray fur would make a fabulous sweater. She carefully collected it in large bags, then spent time carding and spinning. I had to admit, the wool spun from Ben was quite attractive. We discussed at length the spendthrifts who threw their money away on store-bought wool when there was this mine of material thrown out at the local pound. Why had no one else ever come up with this idea? Finally, the Ben-wool sweater was ready. It was a stunning creation, pale gray and white, soft and warm. Talk about proud! My girlfriend was the walking, talking definition of proud.

But there's that old saying about pride and falls . . . The fall came two weeks after the sweater first saw the light of day. It wasn't raining when we started out, but it was overcast; the clouds were dark gray and fairly low. The rain caught us a few blocks from home, and it was a real downpour. We ran to the nearest shop to wait it out, but by then the damage was done. At first I wasn't sure what I was smelling, I just knew that it was BAD. It was only when the other shoppers began to move away from us that the truth struck. My girlfriend's sweater stank to high heaven. Ben the dog, even when soaked, had never smelled so revolting. There was a reason why no one knits dog, and it stood reeking beside me.

I'll gloss over the part where we were asked to leave the store before the merchandise picked up the scent, and the part where we had to trudge home in the sheeting rain. I'll skip to the part where she had to take three showers with strong soap to remove the odor from her skin. I was present when the garbageman picked up her garbage that week and I swear I saw him shudder when he lifted the bag.

So, as a non-knitting observer, I have two pieces of advice for knitters. First: measure your Barbie before you knit. Second: never knit dog.

Greater Love

Susanna Clarke

Big Kitty's discount store holds a strangely central place in my life and the lives of my neighbors. We figure out how to put together outfits from the marked-down racks. We run into friends and acquaintances there and have long discussions among, and sometimes about, the weekly specials. We troll the aisles looking for useful items, like big green soup mugs or cheap smoked oysters or dish towels, 5 for $7.49. You don't go shopping at Big Kitty's for specific things. You go in with an open mind and see what presents itself.

And one day what presented itself was a sale on yarn. Cheap yarn. *Really* cheap yarn.

Now, I am a needleperson only when the spirit moves me, which is maybe once every two-three years, sometimes longer. When the itch hits, I usually hunt out some sturdy twill and sort through my stash of crewels and work out a design. I'm okay at crewel work. I know how it's going to come out.

Knitting is another matter. Of course I learned to knit when I was a child; I remember my mother teaching me. But I am not a good knitter. I dutifully make the sample 4-inch square to make sure that my tension's okay, but once a piece gets beyond those 4-by-4 dimensions, something gives a small lurch-and-shift and my tension goes wonky, usually by a factor of, oh, about 1.1 or 1.2 and always for the bigger. I'm better, but not great, at crochet, as long as we keep it small and simple. Granny squares, fine. Anything larger makes me nervous.

Fortunately the high price of yarn-store yarn keeps me from starting projects that inevitably end up packed into guilt-inducing plastic bags at the back of the hall closet. Back there, unseen but not forgotten, are pieces of a gray mohair sweater—it's a size 10, if you saw me now, that should tell you how far back *that* goes—and an unassembled black oversized tunic-thingie that I really must give to the next adult male gorilla I encounter; it should fit. Also some abortive mittens.

But the racks of cheap yarn at Big Kitty's began to seduce me, a little at a time; I found myself drifting away from the canned tuna to stand empty-headed, gazing blankly at banks of four-ply worsted. There just happened to be a handsome deep leaf-green and a deep blue that begged to sit next to the green; and there also just happened to be a pattern book for sweaters in that selfsame worsted for older boys (size 8–18). I just happened, at that very moment, to have a boy sized 12 who looks to-die-for gorgeous in a good deep shade of green. So many coincidences, all coming together like traffic hurtling headlong toward a three-way intersection . . . I don't remember putting the pattern book and the yarn in my shopping cart. I swear they jumped in there all by themselves. And I swear that they walked me to the cash register and out of the store, before I could get back into my right mind.

Now, this was my downfall: the green-with-blue sweater actually *worked*. I cast on the same way I'd climb onto a bicycle: maybe a little wobbly at first, but getting into the old rhythm almost without thought. After a few inches, I measured the kid's back and measured the sweater's back, and the two coincided surprisingly well, most satisfying. The sleeves were easy to shape. The two rows of blue to start the front, back, and sleeve ribbing and to finish off the neck were a splendid touch. The stockinette I'd worked wasn't, perhaps, as perfectly even as a knitting machine would produce, but that only gave the sweater a touch of authenticity. My son loved the sweater and he looked terrific in it. Watching him walk up for communion at church in my handiwork made my ample maternal bosom swell with pride: see how good a mother I am? With my very own 4.5mm needles I handknit this beautiful sweater for my boy! (Of course, he outgrew it in three months, but that's par for the course.)

Thus foolishly emboldened, I fetched up back at the yarn section at Big Kitty's, and behold, there was another clearance sale on four-ply worsted! How could a body resist? And among the shopping carts of marked-down yarns, there were many skeins of a beautiful clear teal blue. Now, I had a bloke—in fact, I still have him, but we're married now. When I'd first met the bloke, and on many subsequent occasions, he'd been wearing an off-white canvas hat—a real hat, not a ball cap—and a beautiful teal-blue hiking jacket with bits of purple trim, and in that hat and jacket he looked/looks terrific. When, in a thousand years or twenty, he roams God's courts in heaven, he won't be in any old brilliantly white nightie and halo; he'll be in that hat and jacket. God will know a Good Thing when He sees it. I'm sure of it.

And here—on sale, yet!—was teal yarn just the shade of his jacket, well, maybe a little brighter, and purple yarn (not on sale) almost the same color as the trim on his jacket. And there on the rack was a book of patterns for men's sweaters in that very yarn, including a raglan-sleeved cardigan that looked comfortable and undemanding, nothing I couldn't manage. This time, I put the yarn and the pattern book in the cart myself. My right mind never had a chance.

The sweater went swimmingly for the first couple of dozen rows. Then I measured the bloke and I measured the sweater, and it seemed to fit okay, but then I thought, well, he likes his clothes loose and comfortable; maybe I'd better make it a little bit bigger. So I unraveled what I'd knit and started again, size 44 instead of 42. This sweater, being much larger than the kid's green-and-blue number, took longer, but I knit-and-purled diligently and confidently, row after row, two rows of purple ribbing to start with, the rest teal blue, steadily marching on. I was deeply pleased with my progress: all that me-made knitted fabric, agreeably warm on my lap (it was winter) and so beautifully teal. Back, left front, right front, sleeves . . . the piece that formed the neck and cardigan front edges were supposed to be a separate bit of ribbed knitting, but I thought crochet would be firmer, stronger, and more attractive, so I crocheted a long band in half-double stitch, teal bordered with purple, complete with buttonholes in the right places, carefully making it just exactly the right length.

Then I put the thing together: sleeves and front pieces and shoulder seams and side seams, and last of all the crocheted neck band, and I sewed on three brass-type buttons I'd found at the bottom of my sewing box. I was very pleased: the buttons actually *went through the buttonholes*. (You can have no idea how big a deal this is unless you're a very part-time knitter with a long history of failures.) The sweater was done. And the bloke tried it on.

Now, the bloke is 6 foot tall, with a huge rib cage and good meaty shoulders. In his teal-and-purple jacket, he looks both tidy and gently impressive. But the sweater had, without my knowing it, grown as I'd knit it, so that now, instead of being a good comfy 44, it was probably more like a 48, or maybe a scant 52. Anyway, the bloke fairly swam in it. Everything was the right length at least—thank God I'd been careful about measuring the sleeve length! But it drooped on him, bagging wretchedly in the front, bunching up above the cuffs. Even after my careful blocking, every single seam pooched, mostly out but sometimes in, instead of lying flat. And the three brassy buttons looked downright bizarre.

Size wasn't the only problem: the colors didn't work. I hadn't kept in mind that a jacket isn't a sweater any more than a quilt is a bathtowel; what looks good in one can look bloody awful in the other. A high-quality teal-and-purple jacket, created by a good professional designer and made by a reputable firm, is one thing. A homemade teal-and-purple sweater, designed and knit by a rank amateur, is another.

The sweater was like one of those wallpaper or fabric swatches that you stare at in the shop, asking yourself whatever was in the mind of the fool who actually made this up. How could a designer with any sort of professional conscience try to fob this wretched dreck off on an innocent, unsuspecting population? And who in their right mind would ever want to buy it? Or the sweater was the kind of thing you turn up at a yard sale and crow over, laughing and calling your yard-sale companion to come look at your find: "Who the heck ever came up with *that?*" And you tell your friends over dinner about this sweater you found that afternoon—you almost bought it, it was so amusingly horrible—and they all laugh and trade stories about the handmade monstrosities they'd found at yard sales. The sweater was *that* bad.

But the bloke-now-husband wears the sweater—wears it happily and gratefully. He hangs it up carefully, where our four cats cannot reach and destroy it, and when I accidentally-on-purpose knock it off its hanger and leave it on the closet floor at cat level, he immediately hangs it up again, carefully brushing out the dust and wrinkles. He likes it because I made it for him. All I can think is, Greater love hath no man, than to wear a sweater as geeky as this. . . .

When I protest how ugly it is, he says, "I don't care about that. It's a good warm long-wearing sweater. I'm sure it'll last me until the Second Coming."

That's exactly what I'm afraid of.

Please, God, please understand: I didn't do this on purpose. It was an accident, honest. Don't look at it; here, look at this nice crewel embroidery instead, isn't it handsome? No, God, please, please don't hold the sweater up. Just put it down, that's all I ask. Look, I've got a plastic bag here, I'll hold it open, you can drop the sweater in, we won't mention it again. If you'll just do that, I promise not to put it in the garbage; there's still room in the hall closet, with the size 10 mohair and the gorilla suit. Please, God, oh PLEASE . . .

Bodacious Knits

Sir Alexandra and the Lobster Twine

Kim Brody Salazar

My daughter Alexandra has always been fascinated by arms, armor and knights. At 4, she loved watching Laurence Olivier's *Henry V,* preferring it to children's movies. As peripheral members in the Society for Creative Anachronism (we were far more active in our college years than now) my husband and I found no reason to discourage her interest.

For Halloween when she was in kindergarten, Alex asked to be a knight. I instantly thought of knitting mail armor for her. I had made a small bit of the real stuff in my eclectic past, so I knew the drape and weight to aim for. I looked around at knitting yarns and found that even the heaviest of the cottons available were too soft and fluid for my purposes. So I went looking for heavy twine. My search took me to a venerable local hardware store. I found heavy cable-wound seine cordage there. The shop clerk said that the traditional use for twine of this type here in New England was making and repairing lobster traps.

Armed with my lobster twine and US #10 needles, I went home and knit up Alex's coif and hauberk using the garter stitch. The coif looks like a faceless balaclava, with a wide spreading collar around the shoulders. The hauberk is like a long T-shirt, slit front and back at the hem for riding on horseback. To be truthful, I skimped a bit on length for Alex's hauberk as I did not expect her to use it in actual combat. I noodled out the pattern by trial and error, taking notes and eventually posting the working method on my own knitting website.

After I was done, I needed to color the natural ecru twine. I soaked both pieces in a bucket of water in which I had dissolved a couple of teaspoons of black and white acrylic paint. When the mail was dry, I laid it flat and did a few bursts of metallic silver spray paint to pick up the ridges of the garter stitch. When the paint was dry I added a couple of leather laces as the final touch. Alex adored her "chain mail" and wore it constantly. It turns out, though, that the metallic paint took weeks to dry completely, and I had a heck of a time getting silver flecks off polyester bedsheets.

Alex was a particularly fierce knight that first year at Halloween. At the school's holiday costume party, she got into an argument with her principal about who she was portraying. He insisted she was Joan of Arc. She insisted she was Henry V. She also wore the outfit to a couple of Society for

Creative Anachronism tournaments, looking all the world like a hobbit off on an adventure.

Alex is now 9, and has outgrown her costume. The mail now sits in the costume closet waiting for Alex's younger sister, Morgan (now 2), to grow.

We Expected???

Elena Latham Murphy

Many of us have trouble making things for the immediate family but crank out garments with amazing speed for others. My teenage daughter complained royally about this and asked for a rainbow-striped sweater for herself. We went to three local and not-so-local yarn stores to get just the right shades for the color pattern she wanted. She even went so far as to write the colors down in her preferred order. Well, as usual, one thing or another came up and I had to make a few quick gifts for other people. She kept checking my progress on her sweater, complaining one day that she would never be able to wear it this winter. One night she tried the sleeves before I connected them to the body, and pronounced them just the right length but too baggy. When I did have some time to finish her garment I was actually sad to see the end of such a vibrantly colored piece of my work. I carefully blocked it and left it out to dry.

The next day I told my daughter there was a surprise for her downstairs. She did not race down as she would have when she was a bit younger. She very calmly moseyed into the family room with all the élan of a burgeoning teen, stayed a few minutes, then just as casually strolled back to where I was waiting. She thanked me profusely for the sweater, but said it didn't fit right. The entire thing was too loose; it didn't fit her as though she'd been poured into it.

Weeks later, I have yet to see her with her new sweater on. Am I disappointed? YES! Surprised? Not in the least. Teens are so mercurial that I wonder how I could have expected anything different from her.

Oh well; at least I had a wonderful time knitting this rainbow sweater for my firstborn. Who knows? Maybe she will dash out of the door on Monday clothed in that beautiful rainbow—and I will smile.

The Checkerboard Vest

Susan Crawford

Once upon a time there was a knitter who wanted to make a very special sweater for her son, so she rummaged through her stash and found remnants from a dye workshop. They were pretty bodacious colors. She spun them up into a worsted yarn but she still didn't have enough for a sweater, so she rummaged some more. In the darkest corner of her stash, she found some variegated roving and spun that up too. Now, after spinning for months and months, she had enough yarn for the Kaffe Fasset sweater that her son had picked out. She started knitting and spent all her free time working on the sweater, which (after a couple of years) she finally finished. She gave it to her son, who then moved away. The gorgeous sweater was gone. Since she had spent so much of her life spinning and knitting it, she went into a long period of withdrawal.

Then she remembered that she had saved all the little ends she had cut off the wrong side when she finished the sweater. This made for about two handfuls of itty-bitty pieces of yarn. She went in search of this little bit of nothing that she had secreted in her stash. After a long time she found it. She was elated because the colors were just as vivid as she remembered. She got out a pound of white Perendale roving and her drum carder and set about creating a new yarn for a vest so she could wear all the lovely colors that her son had taken away from her. After she had carded all the colored pieces into the white, she spun up the yarn and it was beautiful. She looked all through her pattern books and found the perfect vest for the yarn and got out her knitting needles and started knitting.

This project didn't take her quite as long as the sweater and she finished it in a few months. When she put on her vest she was delighted with the way it fit, and the colors and the warmth that it provided her body. Her son came home from far, far away and she and the gorgeous sweater were reunited because it needed some alterations. After she fixed the sweater, her son put it on and went away, and the knitter lived happily ever after in her new vest.

Stick to It!

Valentina Devine

I grew up in Berlin, Germany, and have been knitting ever since childhood. In fact I don't even remember anybody teaching me how to knit; somebody must have, but I don't remember. I mention the fact that I spent my youth in Germany for a reason. The Germans seem to have a reputation for being very disciplined, frugal and logical. I was told by my father to have realistic goals and then stick to them. How does this relate to knitting? I think anything can relate to knitting!

For me, knitting was always a joy and a relaxation. The joy started by choosing a project, finding just the right pattern, deciding if the design was too difficult to knit and finding the yarn called for in the pattern. I could list at least ten self-created rules that I had to follow in order to complete a project. But I knitted on. And, as my mother had told me, I enjoyed it.

I knitted like that for years, many years; I had children, friends and paying clients who wore my hand-knit sweaters. Then my knitting world changed.

Twenty-odd years ago, I moved to the Washington, D.C., area and met a lady by the name of Joyce Edwards. She taught a class at the Smithsonian called "Free Form Knitting." No pattern, no gauge, no big planning; just bring a few odd balls of yarn and a pair of knitting needles and let it happen. I was sure that this was not my cup of tea! Not for someone like me, who had been raised with a very structured, orderly approach to knitting. I almost left after the first few minutes—but after all, I'd been taught as a child to stick things out. . . .

The beginning was difficult; all that freedom was totally new to me. But after the first two hours or so, the technique got hold of me. It was beyond my control! Instead of agonizing about what color goes with what, I reached into my brown paper bag and used whatever color came to hand. I knitted as many rows in one color as I felt like knitting, broke my strand and reached for a new color. Believe it or not, all colors go together; there is no such thing as the wrong color. The art happens when the knitter is aware of color balance. A row of a very bright color next to a large block of muted color can become a very exciting piece of abstract fabric, especially when you play with the pattern stitch as well.

Eighteen years after taking Joyce's class, I am still knitting abstract garments. I have expanded the possibilities with surface embellishments (crochet or embroidery), I am knitting in every direction possible. My color areas can be linear or round, patterned or irregular. In other words, anything goes. If it feels good, I do it. I have been teaching this freeing technique called "Creative Knitting" for the past eighteen years to hundreds of knitters, in this country and abroad. The wonderful thing for me is that each garment is different. Each person has his or her own color sense; each knitter is a one-of-a-kind designer—and most important of all, each person enjoys the freedom of knitting without a pattern.

In Germany, as a child, I learned how to knit, how to appreciate my yarn, how to make a decision and stick to it. Without those steps, I could never finish a project. But I have learned that there is always room for change and growth and personal joy of achievement. This is what happened to me when I took that class at the Smithsonian—when I decided not to walk out after the first few minutes, but to give it a chance. It was meant for me. I am still enjoying it and passing it on to others.

Knitting Rocks

Pam Kohan

I always experience events and occasions in my life in simple terms: "What can I knit for it?" Whether it is a friend's wedding or birthday, a vacation or party invitation, or even a rock concert, I think of it as potential for a new knitting project. A pregnant woman need only brush up against me and I'm knitting her a baby hat.

But the most famous baby hat that I ever knit was for my favorite rock band. The mere possibility of being able to share something of my passion and creativity with an idol of mine made for one of my more colorful knitting projects. Through a friend of a relative, I was able to get complimentary tickets to a sold-out concert. Being up on these things, I knew the lead singer's wife was pregnant. Little did she know that a distant knitter was about to beat all of her relatives to the punch with the first baby gift to be delivered.

As both a thank-you to my favorite band and an outlet for my desire to "touch the stars," I brainstormed with the bemused knitting group at my local yarn store, Marji's Yarn-crafts. Among us, we designed a funky hat that a rock star baby might live with. The hat is a combination of court jester's cap and little king's crown, knitted in black cotton with a multicolored zigzag edging. Several fantasies floated through my mind as I knit the hat. I saw my hat atop the baby's head in the celebrity column of *People* magazine. I dreamed of a handwritten note of thanks—perhaps a request for more! Or even more gratifying: a moving phone call expressing amazement and thanks—I have rehearsed my side of the conversation, of course. But my ultimate fantasy is the explosive growth of my new website, the trendsetting knittingforthestars.com. . . . All dreams still, as I write. The hat will be delivered at the start of the band's U.S. tour.

The moral of this story: U2 can knit for the stars in your life.

Variegated Yarn

Susan Crawford

I recently returned home to California from visiting my son Scott in Colorado. Mary, a friend who is also a knitter, went with me. I drove 2,330 miles and she knitted 2,330 yards. This trip had two objectives. One was to see Scott and the other was to visit all the yarn stores on the way . . . not necessarily in that order. Mary brought along a book that listed all the yarn shops in the known universe, so we were well prepared for this adventure. The first yarn I bought (on the second day of the trip) was a custom hand-painted merino wool in blue, red, beige, green, purple, and violet. Now, I don't really do variegated. It knits up funny. I've used some in weaving, but it still isn't my first choice for knitting—in fact, it's closer to last. Well, what can I say? The price was right, the colors were fab, the fiber was luxurious, and I guess I lost my mind.

The farther I drove and the more Mary knit, the more that yarn preyed on my mind. I just thought and thought and thought. My first thought was, what on earth possessed me to buy that yarn? My second thought was, I can weave with it . . . but I don't really have anything to go with it right now except a lot of handspun raspberry mohair, and that color combination just wouldn't work. Well, then I buckled down to more rational thinking: What was I going to do with this most irrational purchase? I couldn't think of anything, so I set the problem aside for a while.

The solution really began to jell after Mary started a sweater (her second on this trip) out of some yarn she bought in Durango on the way home. Of course by now I was totally frustrated because she just sat there knitting away while I drove and drove and drove. I wanted to rip the needles out of her hands. Now, don't take this wrong. I love to drive. But I also love to knit. Mary is a good friend; I know she would have driven if I'd asked her to. It just seemed so selfish on my part even to *want* to ask her to drive, just so I could knit. It's okay to ask someone to drive if you are tired or not feeling well, but because you want to knit? No way!

The sweater Mary was knitting had a checkerboard design that was quite appealing. It got me to thinking about THE YARN again. Now, even though I was driving mile after mile,

I also was beginning to think quite positively about my new project. I knew already that the colors changed approximately every 5 inches. That would make a five-stitch pattern. Wow! I'm on to something now. What about a checkerboard pattern—not the one Mary was using, but something similar? What about shape? I had a favorite T-shirt that died a long time ago, but before its demise, another good friend had made a pattern of it for me. I was also thinking about a neck treatment I had seen on a couple of commercial sweaters.

By the time I got home, I had that little puppy all designed in my head and I just had to get it out. I gave my pet bird her treat for the day, dug the yarn out of the motor home, settled the cat on my lap, and started knitting. A couple of days later, after I had finished the back of the sweater, I unloaded the motor home, did some laundry, and looked at the mail. Then I went back to knitting. Seven days later, I think my house is finally in order (as much as it ever is) and the sweater only lacks one sleeve. Next time, Mary is driving!

The Hanah Silk Story

Hanah Exley

For forty-eight years I smoked cigarettes. I started experimenting at eight and was hooked by the time I was sixteen. On October 14th, 1983, at 4:30 in the afternoon, I quit. Within hours I was totally stressed out, pacing the floor, eating everything and wondering why I ever thought I could quit. But I never touched another cigarette after that day.

To keep my hands busy and to relieve the constant eruptions of rage that plagued me, I started knitting as compulsively as I had smoked. Whenever I was awake I knitted. Sweater after sweater after sweater, I knitted. They were all wool, all beautiful, but because I live in Southern California, they were too warm for me to wear. I sent them to my four children, my five granddaughters and friends. Who doesn't love a handmade sweater?

In 1984 I visited Thailand. Bangkok was alive with electric, vivid color. Silks were piled in stacks in the shops. The sensuous colors and feel of the silk awoke in me my own softness, my own sensuality. It was then that I decided to try to knit with silk ribbon. That way, I would make something I could wear. When I got home, I bought five yards of china silk. I hand-cut it into ribbon, giving myself, in the process, a very painful tennis elbow. I knitted it up and immediately realized that as soft and luxurious as it was, the ribbons had to have more liveliness. Off I went to the nearest art store to purchase a few small bottles of silk dye. Although I am an artist, I had never dyed anything. I asked the young salesperson where I could get some good advice. He gave me the names of several silk painters and I called them, one by one. Repeatedly, I was told that what I wanted to do wasn't possible. This negative response just revved up all my juices, challenging me to succeed.

It was at this time that little miracles started to happen. I was discussing with a good friend some of the technical problems that I was facing with my silk ribbon. "Don't worry," she said. "I have an associate who can prepare the silk so that you can dye it." I walked into their shop with some silk and we managed to figure out exactly what to do. After fifteen years I still work with the same company that owned that shop.

I could easily have missed the next miracle. The company that prepared the fabric for me ruined $300 worth of silk. After a lot of bemoaning and blaming, I finally realized that I now had a $300 supply of silk on which to practice. One day, after weeks of experimenting with all kinds of techniques, I made a fabulous ribbon. I named it Earth Mother and to this day it is still my favorite. It is a combination of earthy green, turquoise and lavender. As you can guess, I had decided to make these ribbons to sell. It really had nothing to do with "making money." I just wanted to prove to myself that I could make a saleable hand-dyed ribbon that could be made into unique and elegant sweaters.

The next thing on the agenda was creating some kind of catalogue. For that I would need a computer. I bought a Macintosh and taught myself how to use it. I designed and knitted a vest, a dressy sweater, a shawl and two long coats. I called a photographer whose work had been shown with mine in a gallery and he agreed to take pictures of the garments. The photographs were superb and very inventive, exactly what I wanted. I drew the patterns, wrote the instructions and knitted color samples to put in the catalogue. Now I was ready to sell.

At this time in the U.S., knitting was not as popular as it is today. There were few knit shops, most having closed for lack of business. I had two good customers in LA, but I soon realized it was time to hit the road. I headed for Santa Fe in my car, thinking that it was probably knitting heaven. Wrong! The stores loved the silk, but they wanted the samples reproduced. I was not willing or able to do that. The one knit shop in town said I was too sophisticated for their clientele.

Then the next miracle: I walked into a lovely shop. The salesperson was friendly and very enthusiastic about the silk. She said, "I can't use your product, but you need to meet Luisa. She lives in Taos and hand-dyes wool." Off I went to Taos. I had to wait for her at her knit shop, La Lana Wool, as she was at the annual wool festival, judging sheep. When she returned to her shop and saw the catalogue, she flipped. "My God, do you realize what you've done? No one has ever done this! It's unique! It's amazing! It's marvelous! I love it!" She did get rather carried away, but when a pro flips out, you can believe she knows what she's talking about. With those few enthusiastic words, she gave me the affirmation I needed. I headed back to Los Angeles to work.

During the next few years my business grew and grew, until I was dyeing silk or writing invoices all day every day. At this point I was selling silk ribbons of all sizes to all kinds of stores. I had really perfected my craft. It was time to go national, but I needed help. I called Brooke, my youngest daughter. She lives in Eureka, California, and had owned and operated a potpourri business for eighteen years. I asked her to be my partner. After thinking about it for a couple of weeks ("I've got to be out of my mind to go into business with my mother!"), she said yes. Another miracle: Hanah Silk, Inc., was born. In 1995 my daughter Diana formed Artemis, a company that serves the needle art market. She is the distributor for Hanah Silk. She also offers patterns for knitting, weaving and embroidery. My oldest daughter, Deborah, was asked by a publisher to write a book about making silk flowers. It is her first and is called *The Simple Art of Ribbon Design*.

Hanah Silk is as vibrant and alive as the silks and satins it offers to its many customers. Brooke is CEO, and I am in charge of Product Development and Design. David (Brooke's husband) invents the machinery that makes everything work smoothly. We have added handmade flowers, pin weavings and hand-dyed fabrics to our line of ribbons and have plans for many more products.

I am as excited today as I was the day that the Earth Mother ribbon was born, the child of my continuing love affair with silk and color. The greatest blessing of all is having my family be such a large part of Hanah Silk's success. It is never too late to follow your dreams.

Be as audacious as you want. If it is meant to be, miracles will always happen.

Extreme Knitting

Frozen Toes of Fear

Laurie Doran

It's a cold January day, and I am 850 feet up the steep angled ice, on my second attempt at ice-climbing with a professional guide. I whack the ax into the ice and slowly inch upward. I try to kick the front points of the crampons into the hard, glassy surface. Suddenly my heel lifts out over the top of the ice-climbing boot. I scream, "Rob, my foot just came out of the boot."

"Try to push your foot back into it," he calmly shouts over the howling wind. I try to wiggle my foot back into the boot, but it won't budge. The harder I try, the more the boot moves until it almost goes careening down the cliff. I grab it by the frame of the ice spike and hold on to it. "Rob," I yell, "I can't get my foot back in the boot and it almost fell down the cliff."

"Hold on to it. I'm coming down to help you. Turn your body around so your back is facing the cliff and anchor your ax as best you can and hold on to that boot."

I twist my body around and I gaze down 850 terrifying feet. I feel dizzy and my stomach starts to twist into knots. I must think of something else. I feel my feet getting cold and my toes start to numb. I begin to panic and remember the pictures I've seen of climbers with severe frostbite. Their toes had to be amputated. This won't do! Instead of thinking of frostbite, I make myself imagine that my feet are wearing thick hand-knit wool socks. Then I begin to create the color and design of the socks. My method works. My feet feel the phantom socks, their warmth and softness. My stomach stops churning, and I can feel my toes again.

Just then Rob, my guide, appears in front of me and smiles. I nervously laugh to cover my fear and say, "Rob, I'd like to offer you free knitting lessons for saving my life." He doesn't respond to my offer, but sees my underlying state of panic. He takes off the cloth gaiter that covers my shin and ankle, unzips my outer pant, and grabs the boot. He unlaces the boot, reaches for my foot, and shoves it into the boot. In a matter of minutes, he has laced my boot on tightly, rezipped my pant leg, and refastened my gaiter. He stands up and proceeds to climb back up to the anchor. He secures my climbing rope and tells me to start climbing. Shaking with terror, I unclip the rope from its ring on my belt and remove the ice screw. My hands are trembling so violently that I almost drop the ice screw down the cliff. Somehow I manage to clip it onto my harness. I breathe deep and try to concentrate on climbing. I only have 20 feet to climb to reach an anchor of safety. I muster all the courage I can and forge upward. At last I reach the anchor and Rob. I want to stand as close as I can to him. Suddenly a wave of calm washes over me.

As Rob prepares the rope for a traverse across a ledge he says, "There is a difference between fear and danger. You were not in any danger. It is only your fear allowing you to believe you were in danger." I ponder his wisdom and realize that he kept me safe. I succeed at reaching the top of the climb without a hint of frostbite or a scratch. We rest for a while among a grove of tall pine trees. Then we have a long steep hike down a snowy trail. The sun is getting lower and it is time to go. We arrive back at the climbing school and I again remind him of my offer of free knitting lessons. I tell him that I teach knitting classes and design sweaters. Now my offer makes more sense to him.

Four years later, Rob and I are still scaling vertical routes of ice, and I continue to think about those imaginary hand-knit socks from that day of ice-climbing. I draft out several ideas, but none of them really satisfies me. One day after a climb, I jokingly say, "Rob, we should have matching wool socks this winter."

Then it came to me. I decide to honor Rob, a professional guide, for his dedicated service and expertise for teaching me how to climb and keeping me safe every step of the way. And therefore I make him a pair of hand-knit wool socks that tell the story of our four years of climbing. Each color band in the sock represents a year and every color squiggle represents a major climbing achievement I gained under his guidance. He is proud to own these socks and promises not to wear them out.

On a recent winter mountaineering trip with Rob, I smile

as I pull on my original hand-knit wool socks and nestle into my sleeping bag, remembering the day I gave birth to the idea of making these wool socks. My toes are comfortably warm on this frosty winter night out in the mountains. "Old man winter won't plague me with frostbite this time," I say to myself, and then I drift off to sleep.

Knit One Red Worm

Naomi Dagen Bloom

The image of knitting within the general, nonknitting public is strangely limited.

—Melanie Falick, **Knitting in America**

"You're always a little ahead of the curve," my spouse often comments. It fits, then, that I was the first person in my 1,000-apartment complex to decorate with a compost box filled with red wiggler worms. This was very satisfying—and some neighbors have opted to do likewise. But that alone was not enough for me. Last year I moved on to knitting worms.

No, not knitting with worms as yarn: knitting replicas of worms. It's probably safe to say that I am the first rabid kitchen composter—in the United States, perhaps in the world—who sees knitting worms as the path to saving the earth. When they see my knitted worms, people ask, "So what's that all about?" And every time someone asks, I experience success because this achieves exactly what I had hoped. The questioner has moved deeper into my territory, into my world of my "environmental art," where every question means they are engaged, where my every action brings forth a response from the observer.

Let me back up a bit, through five years of writing, photography, even singing (just once) about the rewards of red-worms-living-with-you, aka kitchen composting, for companionship as well as for solving the garbage-in-landfills problem. This journey began with a performance essay, called "Composting in Manhattan," that I performed in a Korean deli on New York's Fifth Avenue. My essay told of how I discovered that I could give up freezing garbage and looking for a compost site. All I had to do was enhance my apartment decor with an attractive blond wood box in the front hall (doubles as cozy seating for two), fill it with shredded newspaper and vegetable/fruit cuttings, coffee grounds, eggshells. Amazing! The red worms deposited in the box know exactly what to do without instruction.

Kitchen composting is a win-win action, one that allows the composter to feel a personal involvement in making planetary change by replenishing the soil underfoot. My worms reward me every day by leaving behind a nutrient-rich substance known as vermicompost. Called "black gold" in gardening circles, this stuff looks like ordinary dirt. But it's special. It is costly to buy and much desired by people with house plants and by city-dwellers wanting to nurture street trees.

The success of my performance got me thinking about other unexpected ways to spread the gospel. I had time on my hands in retirement. I had no grandchildren to fuss about or knit for. I was pleased to have found creatures besides my cats to worry about. (Too much food? Newspaper too dry? Not reproducing quickly enough?) Cats, those lovers of yarn, are totally disinterested in a covered or uncovered compost box, so our household remained harmonious.

Soon I tried other media. I made a neckpiece with a tiny bag of dry compost, moonsnail shell, copper plant tags, a few beads. "Stunning," people would comment. My crusade took a new turn in 1998, when a group called "Peculiar Works Projects" encouraged me to expand on an installation with performances that they heard I'd put on in Mexico: "*Gusanos, Gusansos Rojos, Viven en Mi Casa.*"

We put on "Worms, Red Worms, Live in My House" (the English title)—five performances in one very long day. In each performance, variations on that first neckpiece became wearable books. Each viewer-participant adorned him/herself with one as part of our "dinner" at a lettuce-covered table. Discarded pantyhose formed cords from which hung recycled plastic containers filled with compost. On red paper was this quote: "The magma circulates through the planet heart and roots suck molecules into biology. We ingest, incorporate, and excrete the earth, are made from Earth. I am that. You are that."

Something struck me about the way that these dinner guests enjoyed touching and wearing the neckpieces. It would take two years for me to turn that realization into the act of knitting red worms. I went to Oaxaca, Mexico, hoping to learn about natural dyeing with local pigments, cochineal (red) and indigo (blue). When this plan went awry, I still wanted to do something with the red wool that reminded me of red worms. Women in Mexico knit mostly on metal needles. I bought a pair of #6 needles and began to use the big skeins purchased in the nearby weaving village, Teotitlan, to create my idea of knit worms. It had been a long time since I had knit; it was easy to return.

Dark red formed the major part of the worm. Yarn from the end of the dye-bath was a perfect fleshy tone to simulate the clitellum, the reproductive part of the worm. Once again, I presented an installation and performance in Mexico—this time with a knit worm on my head. A remarkable education-oriented compost farmer I'd met delighted the gallery crowd with the big box of live red worms he brought, and his explanation of vermicomposting in Spanish. "*Agua y Abono*" (water and compost) opened with my sitting at the foot of a stairway while knitting yet another red worm. People loved touching the worms, wanted to wear them, hold them. It was meant to be.

Back in New York City, I received notice of funding that would support my next effort, the Worm-Ware™ Party, a take-off on Tupperware™. These parties marked the start of the celebration in honor of the closure of the world's largest garbage dump—New York's own Fresh Kills, just across the Hudson from Manhattan. The dump was to close in 2001 and we would knit worms in joy! I wanted to convince other retirees to take up kitchen composting and start a knitting movement. This was my new goal.

Feeling empowered, I quickly wrote a request to a foundation granting funds only to women over 54. Off we went to China. The Worm-Ware box and knitted worms—red Chinese yarn, yellow (their color for earth) for the reproductive part—made a hit in the classroom. I hadn't expected to see so many women knitting in public in Asia—in outdoor markets way north, in Dali, near Tibet, in small shops in Shanghai.

Most of these women were at work on complex designs without printed patterns. Often I'd pull my red worm knitting from my backpack to begin a dialogue with these knitters. Through a translator, we could exchange thoughts about (what else?) worms eating garbage. Our crafts and concerns were mutual.

Back in New York, I got a letter from the Thanks Be to Grandmother Winifred Foundation, awarding me funding for "This Dirt Museum: The Ladies' Room." This exhibition took the Worm-Ware concept further. With this second grant, I proposed to invite courageous women over 50 to free lunches in New York restaurants. We celebrated the closing of Fresh Kills by arranging knit worms on our heads and around our necks and wrists as we ordered. Resting on our table was the Worm-Ware box, the world's smallest composter—a recycled plastic take-out container with real red worms eating garbage, discreetly wrapped in a blue and white polka-dot kerchief with small knit worms on top. Waiters took it for a "cute little Japanese box." Since my first year of kitchen composting, I always carry it and start environmental conversations when people ask what it is. My website, www.cityworm.com, features the Worm-Ware box's many appearances—at the Grand Canyon, at the Great Wall of China, at my daughter's wedding and my son's Ph.D. graduation. My children have a sense of humor, along with a healthy concern for the future of the planet.

Now knitters, crocheters, and felters from all over the country joined the crusade. People from Puerto Rico and England responded to my request to "Knit One Red Worm" for the art installation and performances that marked the end of the Fresh Kills celebration. Contributors were creative in their worm interpretations, their fibers mixed in old men's ties, hemp, yarn, wool—often leftover, but always with some red, meaningful in many cultures besides our own.

New Yorkers were surprised when Fresh Kills closed ahead of schedule. Did knitted-red-worm energy influence City officials? I wondered. Knitting websites and publications, the Craft Yarn Council, and the Big Apple Knitting Guild all delighted me with their support. Lion Brand Yarn donated gorgeous dark red chenille.

"This Dirt Museum: The Ladies' Room" successfully addressed Melanie Falick's concern and introduced many non-knitters to more of the craft than the obvious. Its doors opened October 6, 2001, at Queens Botanical Garden. For three weeks, the plant shop there became an interactive, site-specific, community-based installation with performances. Over 800 visitors could see, touch, and smell compost. They discovered how their neighbors in Queens, the City's most diverse borough, are bringing indoor and outdoor composting into their apartments, houses, restaurants—even a Buddhist temple. I shared my discovery of vermicompost as a new "clay" as we made compost beads and buttons together. There were opportunities to knit more worms and win a Worm-Ware box to take home. All this brought adults and children closer to the sweet-smelling earth and the possibility of making a world of difference through a simple daily practice with red worms.

I'm so glad that I learned to knit from a patient family friend in the 1940s. I wish she were still around to see the 150-plus stockinette-plus-garter-stitch knit worms I made and hear how my love of knitting evolved into this crusade. But that's another story.

Railroading Can Be Hazardous to Your Knitting

Karen McCullough

"Honey, I bought a railcar!!" Little did I know, when I heard that sentence, how my life would change. My husband has loved trains since he was a little boy and is a certified train nut. I have gone with him to ride various tourist railroads and have spent long hours in shops while he debated which model engine to buy. (He rarely accompanies me on my yarn-shopping expeditions!) He'd always wanted to be an engineer and lamented having been born a century too late for the golden age of railroading.

All that was about to change. My husband had made the happy discovery that the railroads are now selling their outdated inspection cars and that ordinary people could buy them. There is even an organization—the North American Railcar Operators Association (NARCOA)—that provides safety information and the like for members. There are meets at which groups of railcar owners/operators can get together and ride the rails (sounds like our knitting guild meetings!). My husband was, of course, ecstatic. He gushed with enthusiasm, telling me that it would be enormous fun and that I could just sit back and knit during the rides.

What he neglected to tell me (he claims that he did not know) was that the rider is responsible for using caution flags at road crossings—popping out of the car to flag down vehicles, for their own safety. I don't know what would happen to the railcar if it were struck by a car but, being a nurse, I do know what can happen to the unprotected flagger! To be fair, during a meet, the cars number off so that the same people are not flagging all the time.

On our first trip, we were number 5, so I had to keep getting in and out of the railcar to flag five railcars through the crossings. This meant that I was getting nowhere with my knitting. Finally, I thought there was a break in the action. I'd just picked up my work when my husband urgently informed me that there was another crossing. I threw my project into my backpack, grabbed my orange flag, and rushed out the door. When we started off again, I reached for my knitting—and watched in horror as it flew out of the open door. It had bounced out of my backpack and was now flying through the air (we were going an unprecedented 15 miles an hour) unraveling the skein as it flew farther and farther behind us. All I could think of was that my wonderful Addi Turbo round needles were going to be crushed under the wheels of the railcar following us and that the whole skein of yarn would be ruined by grease and who knows what else. So I did what any panicked knitter would do—I grabbed at the yarn and started trying to pull it back in. I succeeded in preventing complete catastrophe but my yarn caught on the door of the railcar. My project and needles hung by a thread (literally) from the door only inches from the rails. Of course, there wasn't another crossing for 10 miles so I had to sit there and watch helplessly as everything swung precariously, threatening to drop at any minute. I didn't even have an extra pair of needles to use to start another project from the other end of the skein! When we finally stopped, I took a picture of the hapless project hanging from the door and then gratefully retrieved it. The people in the railcar behind us teased me about the incident (they were taking bets on whether it would stay on the door or fall off).

I thought my knitting woes were over but after lunch, when I was happily knitting (this time I was NOT the designated flagger), I happened to pull more yarn out of the skein than I intended and the strand went flying out the door. Again my project was flying in the breeze, but this time I had no real concerns because my needles were firmly in my hands. But then the yarn started wrapping around the hub of the railcar's front wheel!! The yarn was rapidly being pulled out of the skein. If this went on, I knew my whole project would eventually unravel. I also pictured the wheel locking up because the yarn had gotten into the bearings, causing a train wreck (talk about no protection—there aren't any seat belts in these things). Desperately I grabbed on to the yarn and held very tightly, wrapping it around my hands a few times. Eventually, the yarn broke and I could get on with my knitting. It took me a while to unwind the yarn from the hub when we stopped, but I kept quiet about this mishap. I didn't want the other people or my husband to think that I was accident-prone.

We met a lot of nice people while riding the rails that summer. Some of the other wives also do needlecrafts. I learned to put my project and yarn in a smaller pocket of my backpack and to not pull as much yarn out of the skein. I even got the opportunity to drive (or is it operate?) the railcar while my husband had to get out to flag a few times for me. But I watch my knitting more carefully now and I take along extra needles and yarn—JUST IN CASE!!

Notes from a Nautical Knitter

Lucy Neatby

As a seafaring knitter, I know that many of my personal knitting firsts and significant moments came while I was afloat. Only recently, for example, did I realize that my career as a knitting teacher commenced when I gave my first knitting lesson by VHF radio in the wee hours of the 0000–0400 watch in the middle of the English Channel. As apprentice navigating officers or midshipmen (the lowest form of marine life, apart from the shipboard cockroaches), we were dispatched to sea on any of a variety of cargo ships for voyages lasting four to six months. As part of my pre-voyage planning I would buy needles, yarn, and a pattern that took my fancy to see me through the trip. Fortunately I wasn't as severely smitten with the craft as I am now; otherwise, excess luggage full of yarn, needles, and patterns would have become the norm. I did, however, develop a taste for fine yarn, for greater knitting mileage per unit of luggage space.

Careful project selection on each voyage increased my armory of skills and refined my tastes in yarns. Unconsciously, I became highly analytical about my knitting: with my limited yarn supply there was no merit in haste, and I could spend much time sorting out and refining the small details that the patterns often lacked. If I couldn't figure out the meaning of certain terms, I would grapple with the problem until I had solved it in a way that pleased me. There was certainly no one else aboard with any knowledge of knitting. A project would usually last me the entire voyage.

Sadly, it never occurred to me to seek out yarn shops in ports around the world; I had not yet begun to appreciate my unrivaled opportunities for world-scale stash enhancement. I did, however, develop a taste for ethnic patterns and design, including Moroccan ceramics and rugs, batik from Indonesia, African carvings, Oriental fabrics, and (ironically) African-style printed cloth—a cargo that my ship was delivering from its place of manufacture in the United Kingdom to West Africa.

Having survived my four-year navigation apprenticeship, I took a job as second navigating officer aboard a converted stern-trawler. Our function was to direct shipping traffic around a cluster of barges that were digging an undersea trench across the Straits of Dover—the busiest shipping lane in the world. After I had plied the seven seas from Hull to Hawaii, this was a strange job. We had to bob about and contact passing ships and hope that they wouldn't run us down. The job was best described as long periods of boredom punctuated by spells of total panic. This was the only ship I ever sailed on where I routinely slept with my life jacket ready on my bunk.

I was, of course, ideally suited to cope with the dull periods: I had my knitting. I knit my first shawl aboard this vessel: it was a hideous shade of embarrassed-pink Shetland lace-weight yarn, strangely described as "Natural" on the mail-order form. I recall perfectly the feeling of magic I experienced as I applied the edge and watched the shawl grow into its finished form. I had only one pair of plastic needles with me—ah, the folly of youth! I would knit merrily away on the bridge, sitting above the companionway from the deck below. Periodically I'd drop a needle, which would clatter down the steps, usually losing an inch or so of length in the process. A quick grind in the chart room pencil sharpener and I was off again. By the time I reached the short rows of my shawl, the needle was a mere 5 inches long.

It soon became apparent that I needed a replenishment-at-sea system to support my knitting habit, as I was consuming far more raw materials than anticipated. On this vessel, with her regular home port and shore leave, I could form some sort of rapport with those ashore. I sought out the local yarn shop in Dover and made the acquaintance of a local postman. As a result, I'd make a quick VHF radio call to the pilot station, my friendly postman would collect yarn from the shop and deliver it to the pilot boat, and whenever the pilot boat was next passing the ship, it would deliver the goods.

It was aboard this ship during the night watches that I began coaching a friend aboard another Guard ship as she embarked solo on knitting a baby jacket. "How do I begin the row? Over." "Knit one, then knit two stitches together and knit to the end. Over." It would have been confusing if the pattern had involved any lace! I entered a new phase of my knitting life; with ample knitting resources, I began to knit for anyone who would buy me decent yarn and let me select the design.

This navigating job finished during the stormiest season, when it was too rough for digging. I found another berth aboard a small coastal oil tanker. I discovered afterward that a little reverse sexual discrimination was applied to my appointment: the skipper had five sisters. I owe a debt to his sisters: not only did they educate him well, but once I'd worked aboard this mighty ocean greyhound awhile, they became my clients. The skipper had deep pockets and a sister to fit anything my needles produced. I have fond memories of keeping bridge watches on gloriously clear and sunny afternoons whilst working on a white Aran sweater, having made the liberating discovery that the hood on the radar was the perfect yarn dispenser, keeping the yarn clean and off the deck.

Between knitting and nautical projects I met a handsome engineer, to whom I became engaged by mail (as we were employed on different ships). We met occasionally and both made it to the church on time and were married. The advent of children brought me reluctantly ashore. I was able to ease the transition somewhat by working as a volunteer for the Coast Guard, where my function was to monitor the Channel 16 international calling and distress frequency. This job too involved staying awake at unusual times of night. I of course filled those hours with knitting. Wouldn't you feel more secure knowing that the person monitoring the distress frequency was happily knitting, not snoozing?

part two

fleece, fur, and foreign lands

Mean Reds

Lisa C. Averyhart

The mean reds are horrible. Suddenly you're afraid and you don't know what you're afraid of. Well, when I get that feeling the only thing that does any good is to just hop in a cab and go to Tiffany's. It calms me down right away. The quietness and the proud look of it. Nothing very bad could happen to you there. If I could find a real life place to make me feel like Tiffany's . . .

—Holly Golightly, **Breakfast at Tiffany's**

I know the mean reds really well, but I live a long way from Tiffany's. Take me to a yarn store anytime. . . . Yarn stores are my sanctuary, a place where my creativity flows unchecked and I leave my troubles outside the front door. I don't even need the building itself; it's not four walls and a floor and a ceiling that peel me out of the mean reds. What does it is teaching hands and an inspiring spirit.

The first time I experienced this yarn-store feeling wasn't in a yarn store at all. It was in my grade 4 classroom in my Roman Catholic elementary school. A parishioner had volunteered to teach willing fourth-graders to knit and crochet during a particularly harsh winter (definitely mean-reds time for fourth-graders anxious for recess). She patiently guided our small clumsy fingers as we struggled with knitting needles and crochet hooks, fumbling our baby way through swatches and granny squares, mine all in different shades of brown.

Many grades later, when I completed my first sweater as a high school senior, the feeling only became more intense and satisfying. I had selected a boatneck pattern with geometric shapes and purple yarn—it was the 1980s and I loved Prince. My instructors at the yarn shop were friendly and encouraging. They were always willing to help me read charts and give me advice on how to shape that first sweater. In hindsight, the piece would have been more suitable for an advanced beginner knitter, but with their help, I finished it. I plodded along under their care, dropping stitches, picking up nonstitches, purling instead of knitting, until it was done. I wore that purple sweater with pride and grace. Holly Golightly would have been proud. Visiting that store every Saturday morning and completing that sweater instilled in me a sense of confidence and accomplishment beyond my academic pursuits.

At college I was ready to tackle projects to fight off the Upstate New York cold. To my surprise, a vendor came to the campus college center to sell yarn and beautiful wooden needles. Under her tutelage at her "store"—a table piled high with yarn—I made a variegated purple crewneck with a cable. There were other projects as well. I couldn't wait to visit the "yarn store," where my instructor helped me to hone my knitting skills.

But it was in New York City that I really discovered the respite of a yarn store. As a Midwesterner living in the hustle and bustle of the big city, stumbling upon little shops in the East Village or on the Upper West Side was true serendipity. Yarn stores were my refuge. No pushy salespeople or companions to harry or hurry me; instead, I could wallow in the sybaritic splendor of it all. Touching the merchandise, reveling in texture, was a requirement. When a fabulous new project took shape in my mind, all my senses were engaged.

During graduate school, the mean reds often consumed me. When sketching project ideas in my notes or knitting in class no longer assuaged me, I'd hop into a cab and off to the nearest of my favorite yarn stores, where the mean reds promptly subsided. I was where I belonged. Noro, Colinette and Classic Elite, needles, pattern books and stitch holders would call out, "Hey Lisa, where ya been?" in a heavy New York accent. There together, we knitters united against a world trying to rush us back to jobs, families, class, reality. We bonded over two sticks and string and the fabric we could produce—beautiful in form and function. Even when I was either the youngest or the only African-American in the shop, my yarn-store experience was never marred. I was always welcomed by a smile, encouraging me into the fold. There was the quietness of "groupthink" as we all concentrated on a swatch, a cable or yarn selection. Until, that is, a completed project was displayed or a new technique demonstrated or advice sought on a pattern. Then the place could erupt into OOOOHHHHs and AAAAHHHHHs or "Can I copy that pattern?" or "When that happened to me I increased." It wasn't fame, fortune or profession that joined us but an admiration for the magic that dangled from our respective needles. Through various knitting mishaps, we gathered around to poke, prod, unravel and share similar yarns of terror and triumph. Among discussions of grandbabies, current events, exams or winters in Florida, I learned from a Jewish grandmother never to knit for a boyfriend, only for a husband. Between bits and pieces of our personal lives, we made possible an impossible project, solved a problem, shared a smile. The mean reds became warm yellows and all was right with the world.

Yarn stores are still my refuge easing the mean reds, the blues or whatever. A building or room or just a table, a Tiffany's, where rich fibers and needles await hands and nothing bad could ever happen.

A Bunch of Little Old Ladies

Kay Dorn

The flight from California to southern Florida loomed ahead, so I took out my knitting project—a green tunic sweater for my 4-year-old grandson—and began working the cables.

EDITOR'S NOTE: Kay Dorn reported to us that Barbara "Bobbi" Arestegui, the flight attendant who was part of the Ladybug knitting group, was one of the crew on American Airlines Flight 11, which flew into the North Tower of the World Trade Center on September 11, 2001. May her soul rest in peace.

"Amazing," said my seat partner, "how your hands fly. Have you been doing that long?" It doesn't take much to get me talking about knitting and soon I was telling him about our Cape Cod knitting group. Of course, I knew exactly what he was thinking . . . a bunch of little old ladies hobble into a yarn shop, greeted by the blue-haired shop owner who sits in her rocker clicking needles while the group assembles. They sit in a circle, chatting about yesterday's weather.

If he only knew! This group, which meets at the Ladybug Knitting Shop in Dennis, Massachusetts, is not all old and not all ladies; in fact, not all anything. It is a diverse assortment of lives that come together up to four times a week. We suffer along with beginners awkwardly trying to make sense out of those myriad loops of yarn; and we admire the advanced yarnsmiths who create tiny beaded bags with size 0000 needles. Our knitters include Bob (who makes mittens for his grandkids), realtors, kayakers, antique dealers, homeschooled girls fulfilling their Home Economics requirement, a flight attendant, and (true!) some little old ladies. One of them, Evelyn, came in for knitting lessons at age 82. Now 93, she has her own little ladybug stool to prop her legs on while she knits, perched on a reserved corner seat at our knitting table.

So, far from gossip and small talk, we have an eclectic mix of opinions. We have, for example, decided how Florida should revamp its election process. We've held high-powered conversations on books, retired spouses, hot flashes, health, grandchildren, news events and cooking. And as for that blue-haired knitting-while-she-rocks shop owner, Barbara Prue: the only thing accurate about that description is that she rocks! One day she might be modeling her latest belly-dancing outfit; the next day, she's explaining how she applied the henna curlicues to her feet, or talking about the pleasure she gets from her cello lessons.

We're a diverse group and anything but my flight partner's probable profile. But have not a doubt that knitting is a top priority in our lives. Knitting is what draws us together and what we have in common amidst our diversity. Barbara Prue once said, "The most rewarding people to me are the quiet knitters or someone new to the area who hardly says much at first, but seems to soak it all up. They seem to gain the most from the companionship and new friendships." It is these friendships, which now go well beyond the knitting table, that we treasure so much.

These ties have resulted in people launching adventures they never would have tried alone. They've given strength to the newly bereaved—in fact, our group is often the first outing they tackle as they put their lives back together. We cry for each other at times like these; and we smile with joy when one of us passes around photos of a new baby and chooses yarn for the requisite blankie. Some members of our group have been attending for years; others have just joined and marvel at the closeness of these friends. Some come, solve their knitting problem and leave. Others join us, feel the camaraderie and stay.

Why? Besides a love of knitting, what holds us together? One clue is our instructor, and friend, Nancy Downy. "Special" says it all about Nancy. When she is not busy at her gardener and caretaker jobs, she oversees our knitting groups. She exclaims joyfully at each finished project, and patiently explains, sometimes for the fifth time, how to execute a new stitch. She graciously rips out mistakes, when we cannot bear to do it ourselves, and repairs the damage. We can take on projects that are more complicated or creative than we tackle on our own because we know we can always call, "Nancy, help!" And each day when we leave the Ladybug Shop, we know something new—maybe a different way to cast on or a better way of increasing—all because of Nancy.

Do we need another reason for giving up a trip to the beach or lunch with a friend for an hour in the shop? We're charmed by the rainbow of colors and textures lurking temptingly on the Ladybug's shelves. One knitter brings in the mint-green fuzzy jacket that she's knitting for her granddaughter—and a dozen others love it. "I must make that," each cries, and Barbara traipses up her circular stairway to the storage room and carries down more of that delicious yarn. We also contribute our skills as a group. One year we all made hats and mittens for the homeless; another year we made afghans for Project Linus, to be distributed to terminally ill children.

Our once-a-month birthday cakes have evolved into an every-other-month supper of hors d'oeuvres and dessert. We love meeting the knitters who attend groups on different days than we do, and we get to try delicious new foods and swap recipes. We are grateful for Nancy and Barbara and all those at Ladybug who create this way of life for us—who make the challenge of taking up our needles such a pleasure. They provide the opportunity to meet new friends, keep our minds alert and expand our knitting skills.

So much for little old ladies . . . I thought about the Ladybug as I worked on my cables, and I smiled to myself.

Silent Knit

Shulamith Oppenheim

In the lowest far-right corner of the Letters to the Editor page of the *Times* of London are published each day little gems of English eccentricity. It is the first page I turn to, and I am always rewarded. Many years ago—and how I wish now I had clipped it!—the page had a letter of perhaps five or six lines, entitled "Silent Knit." And what was the author decrying? The disappearance of the wooden knitting needle. Needles that click the click of comfort, of a crackling fire, of a rocking chair by a cradle, the click of warmth and security. Replaced by what? By the waxy plastic needle that makes no sound. An age wiped out, without a click! Happily, wooden needles are back. And my hope is that the woman who wrote those lines nearly thirty years ago is still around and clicking!

From Kathy's Kreations

Kathy Zimmerman

Here at Kathy's Kreations, we've noticed an increase in the number of college students who knit. Several meet in dorm knitting groups in the evening. The most popular projects seem to be accessories, mostly hats and scarves, which require minimal shaping and provide warmth during mad dashes across campus in our chilly Pennsylvania winters. One brother and sister, members of a campus knitting group, stop in my shop periodically. They knit scarves to sell to other students as a way of raising extra spending money and to "support their habit." As I was talking to him, the brother mentioned that he is the only guy in his knitting group. Did that make him uncomfortable? I asked. "Heck, no, it's a great way to meet girls!"

A fairly new knitter came to one of our intermediate classes, determined to make the leap from beginner hats to sweaters with shaping. "I am going to stay here until I get this right!" she proclaimed. She came bearing three Diet Pepsis (caffeine to keep going) and a beer (just in case!).

Found Pattern

Elaine Eskesen

I just found one of my patterns—thank goodness, since a customer wants to make the vest that's hanging up in my shop. I found the written notes quite by accident. I turned over an old envelope while cleaning up my desk and was quite excited to see it there, written down.

I knit whenever I can . . . stolen moments, but rarely stolen in my shop. Customers might comment on *what* I am knitting but never actually see me at it. And this is the way I write down patterns: as an afterthought, something I do at the end of a busy day.

Yet knitting is also a social interaction, it's a commentary about our lives and how we live, while doing other things. The fraction of time, every day, that we are knitting is extremely important. Any knitter knows how it feels to pick up those needles at the beginning or at the end of the day and to create something while reflecting on our daily lives—stitch by stitch, thought by thought, moment by quiet moment.

Knitting is more than an integral part of my life: it is part of my soul, my being. It's been this way for many years. Maybe that's why, fourteen years ago, I decided to open up a yarn store in the summer kitchen in our farmhouse. There my young children could be with me daily. My shop eventually moved into an old building in town. There I began to notice how important the shop was for people who came in. It was a connecting spot for each of them as well.

Coming into a yarn store isn't just about picking out some yarn for a project, it's about reaching out for soulmates, consciously or unconsciously. I had always known this at some level, but it became clear to me one day when a young woman came into my store and started pulling all the orange and red skeins off the shelves (I dye my own yarn so there was plenty of variety). We hadn't really communicated yet. I don't know why I said, "Those are all healing colors." She looked at me and told me that her husband, a police officer, had recently been killed during a high-speed chase. The conversation had begun . . . we reached out and shared part of our lives. That's what knitting is all about. She picked out the colors with no project in mind; that would come when the yarn met her needles in the quiet of her room, after the kids were put to bed.

Dyeing wool every day for my shop is one of my passions. I

consider carefully the colors I choose to mix. I don't write down a formula, I just put dye colors together and create. It's one of the most authentic things that I do. The colors reflect my moods, my daily walks with nature, my passion for life. How people respond to my colors is also very direct and personal; that's why I dye my own. It's a very centering experience. My studio is part of my shop, so any customer can wander in and paint their own yarn or watch me hand-paint skeins of wool.

Choosing colors is also a very personal process. It often takes an hour or two for a customer to create a project. I feel that it's the most challenging part of the process; it requires courage. Any knitter can get confused by all the color choices. If the colors work together, the project will succeed—the knitting is the easy part! I love to help people pick out colors; I also marvel at each person's unique color sense and the excitement that evolves as they work with it. It's like painting with watercolors.

With four almost grown kids and no help in the shop, I can't always be there, and so sometimes the store operates on the honor system. I want folks to be able to look around (especially if they've traveled long distances), to buy wool for a project, or to browse through a knitting book for ideas. Yesterday was an honor system day. I opened my doors at 10 A.M. and put up my sign: "HONOR SYSTEM today. Enjoy my shop. If you want to purchase anything, leave a check in the basket. Thanks, Elaine." Other shop owners in town ask if I get worried about stealing. I say no. Knitters are basically honest, and if someone was desperate enough to steal yarn, I figure they need it more than I do. But I've never had a problem.

Every day is different, as the people who come in talk about their own stories. This is what makes the store so rewarding: it's about them-and-us, our lives, and the common thread of our knitting, which keeps us grounded in our daily lives—that's what fascinates me.

Mercies for the Children (and the Earth)

Winnie's Babies

Scott Morris

LaShandra's eyes lit up and her tears stopped. Her hand stretched out and she started walking toward me. She was fixated on what I was holding: an 8-inch-tall knitted figure of a boy with his hands stuck in his pockets. His shoes were black, his pants blue, his shirt green and his skin brown. I negotiated with my two-year-old patient. We struck a mutually satisfactory deal: LaShandra got the doll and I got to look in her ears. While I told her mother about her daughter's ear infection, LaShandra played in fascination with her new friend.

The same scenario occurs over and over every day at the Church Health Center in Memphis, Tennessee, where we provide health care for the working uninsured and their children. We have over 30,000 patients. That's a lot of knitted dolls to give out.

It all began eight years ago, when I was standing in the back of St. John's United Methodist Church, where I am also one of the ministers. A retired Methodist minister, George McKelvey, and his wife, Winnie, had recently begun attending the church and had taken up residence in the back pew. Before the service began I would talk with them for a few minutes.

One day Winnie asked, "Do you think you would have any use for a few baby dolls in the clinic?" I didn't know to what she was referring. She then reached into her pocketbook and brought out one of the dolls. "I've made these for years for all of my grandchildren, but they are now all grown and don't have much use for them." The doll was incredibly cute. George piped up, "Oh, don't get her started again on these dolls. She spends all her time knitting them." I thought at first George was kidding, but I was soon to learn he was not. Winnie and I talked and she agreed to make a few of the dolls for us to hand out to pediatric patients in the clinic.

Several weeks passed, and I forgot about Winnie's babies. Then one Sunday she whispered in my ear, "Meet me in the parking lot after church. I have something for you." I agreed. After the service I found George and Winnie waiting for me with their hands completely full. Winnie had made dozens of the dolls. It must have taken an incredible amount of time. "I can do this in my sleep. I knit the dolls while I watch TV. It keeps me busy," she said modestly. There were so many dolls I thought it might take weeks to give them all out. But that was before Debbie got hold of them. Debbie Odom is one of our nurses, a woman who truly loves children and loves Winnie's babies. Before I had a chance to use the dolls for my own purposes, I found that a child would have one in his or her hand before I'd even said "Hello."

All was well until one day a mother politely asked, "Do you have one that has brown skin?" I knew the answer. All of the doll's faces were made from tan wool. For years Winnie had made the dolls for her own children and grandchildren. The dolls looked like them, but many of our children had darker skin. The next Sunday I spoke to Winnie about the problem. She began to think. "I don't have any brown yarn but I bet I can find some." A couple of weeks went by, and before church one Sunday, both George and Winnie could hardly contain their excitement. Winnie, with a big grin, said, "I've got something for you." After church they presented me with dozens of new dolls. They looked exactly the same—just as cute, with the doll's hands in its pockets, and with brightly colored pants and shirts, only now the faces ranged from light tan to dark brown. There was truly a "baby" for every child.

I can't tell you how many dolls Winnie has knitted. From time to time a sack of dolls appears on my office chair at the church. Occasionally George shows up unannounced with a special delivery package. He will only leave Winnie's babies with my assistant. "I don't want to have to face the music if I can't account for making the delivery," he says, laughing. He knows he is a part of this special gift. Some families with four or five children have been given one of Winnie's babies for every child. But every time it is the same. The crying stops, the child's eyes open wide, her hand reaches out, she takes the baby into her own hands and looks at it in the face. A face that reflects her own. It is a wonder to behold.

Machine-Knit Mercies

Christine Cooper

I am a member of Haslington (England) Knitting Club, which was formed about ten years ago. During this time we have always tried to knit for our local premature baby unit, since small items of baby clothing are almost impossible to come by and would be very expensive if the hospitals had to purchase the amounts they need.

I was lucky; when I had my first daughter, who weighed 5 pounds 8 ounces, my mum knit everything for her by hand, just as she had done for me when I was a baby. Mum knit everything from the little vests my daughter wore to the gown and shawl she was christened in. When, three years later, I had twin daughters, Mum did it all over again, this time in duplicate. One of my twins was taken into the special care unit, at Leighton Hospital, Crewe. The baby was fine, but just a bit small, at 4 pounds 6 ounces. In those days they put all babies under 5 pounds into the special care ward. (The other twin was over 6 pounds.) That was the first glimpse I'd ever had of *really* tiny babies. Mum began to knit for this ward as well, making little cardigans and pairs and pairs of tiny bootees. Now in her 80s, Mum still goes on knitting. She says that if she only had one ball of wool, she would keep knitting it up, unraveling it, and knitting it up again. I have always known from a very young age that if you are a dedicated knitter, you are well and truly hooked.

There was no way I could keep up with my mother's knitting without help. So about nine years ago, I bought myself a knitting machine and joined the local machine-knitting club. It had just been formed and had received a generous grant of £250 from the Cheshire County Council. We used the money to buy a secondhand knitting machine for club use. We felt that since we had been given such help, we'd pass this help along to others. Since then, the club has sent knitting machines to Romania and raised funds for all sorts of good causes.

The club has always knit for the neonatal unit at Leighton Hospital. One day, we got a letter from the hospital explaining that they were trying to purchase a new MRI scanner, which would cost about £1,000,000. Would our club be prepared to try to raise £100 for their appeal? We agreed, and we recruited the nearby Sandbach Knitting Club, with which we shared some members, to join us. We held a Coffee Evening with a stall, sold some of our knitwear, and easily raised the £100. Then we just kept on going. When we'd raised a few hundred pounds, we thought we'd try to raise £1,000. "Much wants more," as the saying goes, and this is how we felt. Some of our members really had the bit between the teeth. We recruited still other hand- and machine-knitters from the area. With the hospital's blessing, once a month we set up a stall in the main outpatients' department, selling knitwear and knitted toys. Our contribution in the end was almost £6,500. What is more, we'd enjoyed the challenge and made a whole new circle of friends.

Whilst the MRI scanner project was still ongoing, we came across a pattern for a little ventilator bonnet (baby cap) with a flap on top. We could see that with a few alterations and refinements, it could be useful. The pattern was for hand-knitting. Although we are a machine-knitting club, nearly all of us hand-knit as well. One of our ladies knit up a prototype, and I took it into the neonatal unit at Leighton. The look on the nurse's face when I showed it to her was a picture. She said, "I can't tell you what a difference this will make! Sometimes we try to cut a hole in the top of the baby bonnet, but of course the stitches run." The nurses were thrilled with the prototype. It would let them examine the baby's fontanelle with the least possible disturbance.

We rewrote the pattern completely, added the necessary changes, and sent photocopies to our local neonatal unit. After much publicity in the local press and on local radio, we asked if anyone would be willing to knit a few of the bonnets, as we now had a pattern for both hand- and machine-knitting. Ladies from all over our area offered to knit—bonnets, bootees, cardigans, blankets, anything in the baby line that the hospital needed.

May arrived, and Crewe and Nantwich Borough welcomed a new mayor, Ray Stafford. Each new mayor chooses a theme for their year in office and Ray chose "Unity in the Community." He wanted to encourage people to give their time as well as their money to local groups and organizations. Well! We could identify with that.

One of our members is the wife of the chairman of our local branch of the Royal Air Force Association. We thought what a good idea it would be if we brought young and not-so-young together at a garden party. The mayor and mayoress opened the party for us. We had an excellent time and raised more than £600, to share between the neonatal unit and the R.A.F. Association.

We were now firing on all cylinders. Could we do a Christmas project? Yes, we could: we knit a little set of garments plus a tiny stocking and toy for every newborn baby in the hospital over Christmas. We contacted Numark Pharmacies and they very kindly donated a tube of hand cream and a tablet of soap for every mum in the maternity wards at Christmas.

We knew that we could not possibly let all these enthusiastic knitters just disperse. We decided to form a knitting circle and asked the mayor if he would be willing for us to incorporate his name in the title. And so the Haslington Ray of Hope Knitters Circle was born.

The hospital told us that they hoped to develop a transitional care unit, to care for babies who need special but not intensive care and which would keep mothers and babies together. Perhaps we could help with new window and bed curtains? We put out a plea and soon had offers of sewing. We have now finished all the bed surround curtains, have almost finished the window curtains, and have made and hung some blackout curtains on a different ward.

Our wonderful knitters keep their needles going. We now have a stall twice a month in our hospital's outpatient department. To date, with donations and sales, it has earned £2,700. We have, of course, gone on supplying the neonatal ward with all it needs in clothing, small blankets, crib sheets, and the like. The pleasure some of our older knitters get is enormous. They love to knit (it's an addiction, you know!) and they know their skills are wanted and appreciated. We put out appeals for wool when we can. If we get any wool unsuitable for babies, some of our ladies knit or crochet it into blankets and bed socks for the stroke ward, so nothing is wasted.

We invite anyone to join us for fund-raising, for coffee gatherings, morning get-togethers—anything that brings local communities together. It needn't be a grand affair; every little helps, even 10 pence. All we ask of people who want to join us is that they meet certain criteria. They must:

1. Want a baby;
2. Have already had a baby; or
3. Have once been a baby.

If they can answer "Yes" to one or more of these criteria, they are eligible to join.

This has only strengthened a belief I've always had. Knitters—what a wonderful breed! God bless you all.

The Cap Project

Betty Meakim

Our Knit-a-Cap project began in 1968. It was started by two Vassar College professors, Dr. Helen Van Alstine and her close friend, Dr. Dorothy Levens. Both had spent some time on Indian reservations and had noticed that Native American children were having problems with ear infections. Helen, a medical doctor, came up with the idea of knitting caps for the children.

In that first year, the project knitted only 58 caps, but it soon blossomed. There were ups and downs, but in some years, knitters produced more than 3,000 caps. Helen and Dorothy recruited knitters from all over the United States. After the founders retired and moved to Lenox, Massachusetts, other knitters dropped out of the project due to illness or old age, and some schools had to be phased out of the project for lack of caps. After Dorothy died, Helen felt she could no longer keep the project going, and so I volunteered to take on the project.

The knitters we have now range from young mothers to women over 90. They are delighted that the project is continuing, because not only does it keep their hands busy, but it helps our Native American children. We ask only that our knitters follow instructions and make the caps colorful. In the past, some knitters sent their work directly to the schools or missions, but now we prefer to collect the caps here in Hadley. It helps us keep track of our ongoing list of recipients, the number of caps sent, and the replies received.

We collect the caps in September. When we pack them, we try to put caps from several different knitters in each parcel, so that there's a variety of colors and sizes going to the same school. As you might expect, some of the schools in mountainous areas have snow and very cold weather early in the fall and are glad to get the caps almost as soon as school starts.

The letters we get back from these schools—some with photos and hand-drawn pictures—are delightful. Some schools let the children keep the caps at home; others hand them out at recess. One teacher said that she was using caps that we'd sent three years before.

In the fall of 2000, we sent 1,963 caps to 45 reservations (Navajo, Hopi, Lakota, Blackfoot, Sioux, Crow, and

Cheyenne). We're trying to recruit more knitters. If you are interested, please contact me at: 143 Mt. Warner Road, Hadley, MA 01035.

Twenty Years and Still Growing

Margaret Klein Wilson

Step into the retail shop of the Green Mountain Spinnery in Putney, Vermont, and you are immediately struck by the sweet peaty aroma of fiber, a vivacious array of color and texture, and the sense that you are in the middle of something wonderful. That sense is not mistaken. Step beyond the shop, and you are surrounded by the stuff of making natural fiber yarns: bales of raw wool, carding and spinning machinery, scouring and finishing systems, and more. Spinning and knitting, fleece and fiber are the staple conversation among fourteen full- and part-time staff. In the late 1970s, the lack of local yarn made of natural fiber set Claire Wilson and Libby Mills, both weavers, on the path to opening a spinnery. "There was a gas shortage," Libby recalls. "Most yarns were either imported or petroleum-based." Claire and Libby thought that making yarn locally from regional materials would conserve petroleum resources two ways: minimal fuel would be used to import materials, and natural fibers would replace oil-based synthetics.

(Reprinted from *Interweave Knits*, Fall 2001)

At the same time, David Ritchie and Diana Wahle, graduate students at the School for International Training in nearby Brattleboro, were in a study group with Claire examining how individual choices of every kind related to global issues. At the center of their discussion was E. F. Schumacher's *Small Is Beautiful: Economics As If People Mattered* (Harper & Row, 1973). The book spoke directly to their concerns about the shift in Vermont's economy from agriculture to industry and tourism. David remembers, "We wanted to work in ways that best reflected living in harmony with the earth, using local resources to sustain a local economy." The idea of a spinnery suited them all, though none had ever run a business or worked with heavy machinery. (Understand that Putney is home to several progressive educational start-ups, orchards, agriculture, and a thriving artisan community; in short, it's a place where Birkenstocks have always been in fashion.) The group envisioned a facility where New England shepherds could sell their fleece or have their fiber spun into yarn for value-added products. Their goals were all of a piece: to use natural fibers to make high-quality yarns in environmentally sound ways while supporting local agriculture.

"We had a growing source of raw materials," Libby explains. The Vermont sheep population boomed from 8,000 to 26,000 during the 1980s as small wool flocks replaced less profitable dairy herds. "And wool," Libby points out, "is a renewable resource." The value of renewable resources—and the overall concepts of reuse and recycle—were new and radical in 1979, she recalls. Today over 18,000 sheep keep Vermont's meadows, hills, and ski slopes grazed and green.

The intrepid foursome acquired loans from state agencies and numerous friends. And in December 1981, the business opened, ironically in an abandoned gas station on the interstate. A barnlike addition created space to house the early 1900s carding, picking, and spinning machinery purchased from textile mills in Maine and Massachusetts. "The first year," Claire remembers with some amazement, "was wild. We all had to learn everything about making yarn with these machines."

Three of the four owners remain today, continuing in their founding roles. David manages the purchase and evaluation of all fibers and supervises each step of the yarn-processing. (Over the years he has worked with more than thirty different fleece breeds individually or in combination with precious fibers, including alpaca, llama, angora, organic cotton, silk, and even wolf hair.) Libby, retired since 1992 from the Putney School as dean, teacher, and director of the weaving program, and Claire, a journeyman weaver, collaborate on every aspect of yarn, color, and pattern design. All three share in marketing, company administration, and the challenges of maintaining sound environmental production practices while making what one of their customers fondly calls "yarn that is real yarn."

Half the spinnery's business is spinning their label yarn for wholesale and retail customers nationwide. All Green Mountain yarns begin with clean, domestic natural fibers. Unlike most commercial mills, Green Mountain does not use any chemicals to mothproof, shrink-proof, or bleach the materials. The care taken in making each yarn, spun in small lots, is evident in its hand, texture, and even aroma: lively, supple, and distinctly "natural."

The first Green Mountain yarns were 100-percent wool sport and worsted-weight in natural and gray ragg. "What a great surprise to discover that our customers were knitters, not weavers," Claire laughs. "They wanted lots of color and patterns." Today the spinnery produces nine varieties of wool and blends of wool and precious fiber in over fifty-five dyed and natural colors. A consortium of friends, local artists, and staff design projects to support the yarns. The patterns are classic, simple, and elegantly practical. "We design sweaters for every level knitter, sweaters we want—and need—to wear," Libby notes as she puts the finishing touches on the test model of a new pattern.

Creating custom yarns for small fiber producers, fiber artists, blanket weavers, and knitting designers from Maine to Montana comprises the other half of the spinnery's business. "Our custom projects nudge us into new territory," David says of the challenge of creating highly specific, out-of-the-ordinary yarns for a diverse client list that includes artist Kathryn Alexander, The Atlantic Blanket Company, Montana's Thirteen Mile Farm, and the ESPRIT clothing company, for whom David developed a non-petroleum oil for carding and spinning. His process, dubbed GREENSPUN, is an alternative choice for people with chemical sensitivities, and David's work encouraged NOFA (the Northeast Organic Farmer's Association) to develop organic standards for processing yarn.

Looking back, Claire speaks for all three owners. "We are so grateful to be doing work we love." Looking ahead, David recalls the spirit of the spinnery's idealistic founding in 1981. "Keep your eye on the overall view, and work through the details in a relevant way. Gracefully." New goals include finding more uses for waste wool, investigating the possibility of turning Green Mountain Spinnery into a worker-owned co-op, and fine-tuning the new wastewater filtration system.

To mark its twentieth anniversary, the Green Mountain Spinnery produced a new catalog in 2001. "From Our Hands to Your Hands" is a tribute to the vision and purpose with which the company was founded and from which it continues to grow.

All Creatures Great and Small

Wolf Scarf

Luis Tovar

Jennifer sat across the kitchen table from me: a small woman with long, flowing blond hair, sparkling blue eyes, and an infectious laugh—an independent woman who enjoys work and the humorous aspects of life. Behind her, through the kitchen window, I could see large cottonwoods bordering the lazy brown Rio Grande. To the left were wolf-proof fences behind which a pack of ten gray-and-black pups were playing. The aunt of the pack kept a watch while the alpha male and female were kept in separate pens.

"The bigger ones are beginning to shed," I noted.

"Yes." Jennifer smiled and sipped her green tea. "It always happens in spring." She laughed. "Once I had the brilliant idea of collecting wolf fur and spinning it into yarn. I felt like Gandhi spinning away, making my own yarn. It kept me busy during the summer months. I collected enough to make a small ball of yarn. Blending it with some like-colored wool, I had enough to knit a scarf. The idea of using sheep's wool and wolf hair in the same scarf intrigued me. The combination of the docile, peaceful lamb and the cunning, strong wolf . . . it made me pine for Clovis."

"Are you still in love with him?"

"Hardly!" She laughed. "Our separation was messy. But it occurred to me that what we had was a fire-hot slippery kind of passion. That was something I missed. Anyway, I thought that as a gesture of goodwill I'd send him a birthday gift. A friend told me that he'd complained of the bitter winter winds up in New England. The scarf was something he could wear. I could entertain images of him in his blue jogging outfit with my gray scarf around his neck. It would flap in the wind as he crunched through the snow-covered forests of Maine. The dreaminess of it all was just a romantic side of me. But it quickly turned sour."

"What do you mean?"

"Oh, the gift arrived just in time for his birthday, in November. I even took the time to find special paper to wrap it in. I heard that his two dogs growled and scratched at the box it came in. He couldn't understand their behavior. When he finally opened the box and pulled out my scarf, the dogs lunged at it and tore it to shreds. I suppose the wolf scent set them off." Jennifer paused then began to laugh again. "Can you imagine him jogging with a pack of dogs barking and trailing behind him, snapping at his neck trying to get hold of the scarf? My scarf could have been his death!"

I laughed nervously.

"To this day," Jennifer went on, "he thinks my gift was an attempt on his life. I terrify him now!"

I eyed her with admiration. She smiled back at me, knowing full well the effect this story would have on me.

I still enjoy Jennifer's company, on occasion. But before I ever wear a scarf she's made for me, I test it on my fearless Chihuahua. If the dog attacks it or runs away in fear, you'd better believe me—I won't be caught dead wearing it.

Mom, Molly, and Me

Bridget Arthur Clancy

I didn't grow up in a household where we made a lot of our own clothes, grew our own vegetables, or were good at do-it-yourself home improvement projects. There might be the occasional try, but nothing was a regular practice. My mother was not much for crafts. She knew how to do embroidery, and when my oldest sister grew up she taught us how to do needlepoint. But knitting—no.

For the last eight years or so of her life, my mother suffered from bone cancer. She had to walk with a cane and wasn't able to move around easily or to go places as much as she used to. If she had to be out for any length of time, she needed to use a wheelchair. As time went on, she had to depend more and more on the wheelchair and on having someone to help her get around. This was an alien existence for my mother, who had never been one to sit still for a very long time. She picked up needlepoint again, and stayed with it until she went to visit her cousin in Florida one year. The cousin taught her how to do counted cross-stitch and bought her a lot of supplies to get started. Counted cross-stitch then became her constant companion. She made beautiful things, which she loved giving away to friends and family. Whenever she would come to visit us, she would bring a few projects with her.

Our gray tabby cat, Molly Bloom, thought counted cross-stitch was fascinating: all those string-type things! And the up/down movements were so exciting. She would wait until my mother got started and then she would suddenly attack the floss, wreaking havoc with my mother's nerves and her project. My mother would say, "Bridget, what's wrong with this cat?"—though with as much amusement as irritation. Once Molly was finished getting into trouble, she would jump up on the chair next to my mother, and sit with her for hours, purring. I think Molly loved the fact that she could attract some attention and then spend the rest of the time being a companion and "helper." Since my husband and I were usually at work during the day, Mom and Molly kept each other company, and got a lot of counted cross-stitching accomplished.

My mother died in 1988, and for awhile Molly had no crafting companion. I knew needlepoint, and my mother had taught me counted cross-stitch, and though I enjoyed both of them, I only worked on my projects occasionally. But in 1992, we bought a house in Center City Philadelphia, and one day while I was out walking around the neighborhood, I came across a yarn store. I had briefly learned the very basics of knitting years before and had knitted garter-stitch scarves for my mother and my husband for Christmas that year. I'd enjoyed knitting, but I had lacked easy access to supplies, and no one else I knew was interested in knitting. So that was that. Well, here I was, in a neighborhood with a yarn store! I went in and added my name to their mailing list, hoping to sign up when they offered beginning knitting classes.

About a year later, I got the chance to learn to knit. I was hooked in no time flat! Granted, I was (and still am) a very slow knitter, but it was so much fun, and so engrossing, that I wanted to spend all of my spare time knitting. By this time, we had four cats, Molly being the oldest as well as the one in charge. She was so thrilled that I had taken up knitting, since it involved not only string-type things but also interesting (and apparently tasty) needles. Better yet, it made me sit in one place for a while. Every time I would sit down to knit, she would be right there. We would go through a brief conflict, where she would grab yarn and/or the needles, and I would take them back and tell her no, and then we would settle into a pleasant routine of knitting (me), and purring (Molly). The other cats would be briefly interested, but usually not to the same extent.

I realized that I enjoyed my knitting sessions with Molly by my side, not just because she was the best and sweetest kitty in the universe, but also because it reminded me of my mother. It would bring a smile to my face to think what my mother would say if she could see Molly glued to my side, purring, as she used to do when my mother worked her cross-stitch. Often I felt as though the three of us were sitting there, enjoying each other's company.

When our cats cuddled with us, we always said they were

"nozzing," though I'm not sure where we came up with that term. My knitting and nozzing sessions with Molly became a special part of my day, and (I think) of hers as well. I would talk to her and sing to her, and she would respond by purring, nozzing, and occasionally, drooling. I told her we were the founding members of the Knitting and Nozzing Club.

Molly Bloom died in January 1999. I still enjoy knitting, and usually have one or two projects under way, which take an inordinate amount of time, since I still knit so slowly. The three cats who knew Molly, and another that we have adopted since then, take an occasional interest in my knitting. They do like to sit with me when I am working on something, and I enjoy their company. But it's not the same as the meetings of the Knitting and Nozzing Club, and it will never feel like it did when it was Mom, Molly, and me.

Winter Birth

E. Anne Mazzotta

My parents, Matt and Amelia, grew up together in a small village in Newfoundland. They moved to the capital, St. John's, thirty miles from their homes, during their teen years to seek employment. The effects of the Great Depression were everywhere. They worked in St. John's until they reached their late twenties, at the end of World War Two. After a long courtship they decided to marry and to leave the city and start their new life in a small community to the south. The economy of the village was based on the fishery, mainly cod but also mackerel, halibut, salmon and lobster. They were married in August and moved immediately into the house Matt had built. For employment they decided to open a small grocery store. They would also stock merchandise that would be needed by fishermen and their families, such as bulk salt, fishing gear and household items. They also decided to purchase a cow.

All went well their first few months. Then, to their great delight, Amelia found out she was pregnant. The baby was to be born in June. The business did well and Matt started growing some vegetables on land he had purchased not far from their home. Amelia kept very busy, knitting, sewing and tending the store. Their little cow, Holly, was also found to be expecting. Life was certainly good for the young couple. Their first Christmas together was very special and they had many visitors to their new home.

One particularly cold night Matt went to check on Holly. The cold Atlantic Ocean roared in the background. As soon as he entered the stable, he knew something was wrong. Holly was giving birth prematurely, on one of the coldest nights of the year. Matt and Amelia were at a loss about what they should do. Matt went to fetch an older neighbor who had a lot of experience with animals. The situation looked bleak. The old man said the young calf wouldn't have much of a chance to survive. The little calf was delivered but was in serious trouble. Its breathing was labored and it was suffering from hypothermia. The cow made no attempt to feed it so Matt gave it small amounts of milk by hand and it feebly sucked on his fingers. But the newborn's temperature was still falling. That is when Amelia came up with a plan. She ran into the house and came back with a pure wool coat sweater she had just finished knitting for herself. She put it on the little calf and almost immediately the newborn stopped shaking. Matt and Amelia continued to feed the calf by hand for quite some time. The little calf wore the sweater until it was out of danger, and it grew into a strong cow. Amelia never regretted the sacrifice.

The Consolations of March

Margaret Klein Wilson

One fellow farmer says that March in Vermont is like November in that you just never know what it will be like. One year it's subzero with storm piling on storm; the next year it's all formless freezing drizzle. But the main problem with March is that it's not quite winter and it's not quite spring and all you can do is wait out the weeks in between. By late winter, chances are you've read all the books you received over the holidays and you've been to one too many potluck dinners. Sunshine is scarce and the snow is old. The best sap has run and been boiled into syrup. No amount of abject mooning over seed catalogues will hurry up the thaw. In your heart of hearts, you know there will be nothing remotely green or emerging for at least three weeks.

Thank goodness for little lambs. During the grimmest, grayest month of the year, watching them is a fine distraction. The liveliest place around is the lambing barn. By the first week in March, the last lambs of the season are being born. What was miraculous in late February—those first births with every nuance pondered and recorded—has turned into a comfortable routine. The initial exhaustion and anxiety of the first weeks of lambing has settled into healthy fatigue and a sense that all will be well. I still hurry uphill to the barn every morning and several times during the day, not to witness a birth, but for other reasons.

Once a ewe has lambed, she and her lambs are cajoled away from the birthing site and into a four-by-four short-walled stall called a "jug," where they will spend the next three or four days. Being penned in this small space helps the bonding process along and makes it easy to identify and handle lambs that might need special attention. The jug also makes it easy to do some close observation without disturbing them.

The antics of young lambs could make a stone smile. Lambs make the transition from being tentative newborns to energetic and highly comedic young animals in a matter of days, making for one of the sweetest and shortest seasons in this farm's year. Newborn lambs charm you with their bleating determination to stand and find food. They wobble around their mother, trying to stay upright while she licks them relentlessly, erasing every scrap of afterbirth. In the meantime, the lamb is probing any dark crevice looking, calling for . . . well, *something*. When a lamb finally does figure out how to nurse, it nearly blooms in front of your eyes. Little wet ears perk right up and out, looking more like helicopter blades than body parts. Their tiny bellies swell after each nursing, and then they fold their impossibly long legs underneath them and settle in the straw to rest. Wrinkly and dazed, they peer around briefly before dozing off.

By the second day healthy lambs are nursing confidently, tottering around, and then curling up next to the ewe for warmth. Their fleeces are dry and whitening. They explore the perimeter of the jug, nibble at the ewe's hay, and poke their noses through the slats of the stall to investigate who and what is on the other side. Sheep are, after all, flocking animals. They are happiest in a group, and lambs are immediately interested in their extended families.

But perhaps most amazing to lambs, and appealing to anyone who is watching, is what happens on day three. The lambs discover that their legs will not only carry them forwards and backwards, but upwards. The first time they hop, or "prong," is usually by accident. Pronging is a particularly sheepish sideways, hop-twist-and-kick move, and it stops them dead in their tracks. It is not hard to imagine what they are thinking at this moment: "WHAT was THAT?" quickly followed by, "How can I do it again?" And they do, over and over, leaping and twisting—astonished, joyful, delighted at what their bodies can do—until they are dizzy and panting. Multiply this scenario by a dozen or so and you have your own in-house circus.

Once the lambs and ewe are released from the jug, the lambs must adjust to the momentary chaos of being in the larger pen with a crowd of older lambs and ewes. There is a brief spell of wailing and WA-AHH-ING! until they find their mother. A moment of frantic nursing ensues. That done, they start to get acquainted with the other lambs and return to perfecting their pronging, quickly discovering they can run and prong at the same time.

Once one lamb starts to prong, they all join in. Moving in a wave, the lambs careen back and forth, bumping and racing up and down the forty-foot length of the pen, reveling in their physical prowess. A bale of straw centrally placed in the pen becomes a launch pad, an ideal spot to jump onto and away from. Leap, land, twist, and fly. With each try lambs gain more height while executing this maneuver. It is not uncommon to be in the shepherd's room next door and see a lamb sail past the window. Whoever coined the phrase "growing by leaps and bounds" must have been a shepherd.

The lambs' surprise and pleasure in being able to levitate—*this* is the local antidote to the end-of-winter blues. Friends and neighbors and children make regular treks up to the barn, counting on the lambs to provide a little comic relief, to bridge the season between seasons. Usually the lambs deliver. You can't help but laugh, and keep watching, and forget that outside it is still March.

Peaceable Fleece in Foreign Parts

Peace Fleece

Peter Hagerty

It was early evening and the monks had begun lighting the thousands of Christmas-tree bulbs that covered their island monastery. "So the American bomber pilots can see us," one monk said, and smiled as he shuffled by. The Mekong River, a dull brown soup of mud with an occasional stick, slowly flowed by on its way south. Viet Cong patrols set up their night ambushes somewhere on the opposite shore. It was the summer of 1970 and the Vietnam War continued on relentlessly.

"What if the clouds come in and the pilots can't see the lights," I asked in French. "God sees through clouds," said the monk as he shinnied up a tall pole to replace a lightbulb.

An American journalist had asked me if I would like to visit an extraordinary Buddhist monastery on an island in the Mekong River, the home of the Dau Ur, or "Coconut Monk." I agreed readily. I knew I needed a break from my work in Saigon. I had come from Southeast Asia as an ex–Navy officer who had refused combat orders. Having spent much of the previous year fighting in my own defense, I was now free of the military and able to spend time helping other American soldiers do the same: I worked in an Army prison south of Saigon, helping these men prepare for their day in court. For hours I listened to what the war had done to the lives of these soldiers and could only imagine what it might do to their future.

The B-52s began their bombing run after evening prayers. The bombs shattered the jungle and made their way out into the river, marching like a giant water monster toward the monastery's lighted towers. Then they hopped the island and made their way toward the western shore. I lay awake for hours on my straw mat, listening to the monks chanting and the waves lapping, waiting for the pilots to return. Sometime after midnight I heard a small engine pushing a dugout canoe arrive at the island. Four men in black pajamas and flip-flops stacked their weapons in the boat and made their way up the path to the monastery. These men were the Viet Cong.

"*Bon soir,*" I said in my schoolboy French. "*Bon soir,*" they replied. As we talked, I came to realize that these were the communist soldiers I had been trained to kill, with bayonets, with rifles, with artillery. They had come to see the Coconut Monk, their spiritual adviser. They were young, maybe fourteen. Had they also been trained to kill me? "Do you know the fate of José Rodriguez?" one asked. He smelled of wood-smoke and his teeth were blackened from the nuts he chewed. Who was Rodriguez, I asked myself, a Cuban political prisoner rotting in some Miami jail, perhaps a leader of a California farmworkers union? I was embarrassed and quickly growing afraid. "I'm sorry," I said in French, "I don't know José Rodriguez. Who is he?" "He is due to pitch for the Yankees tonight in the third game of the World Series and your Armed Forces Radio says his arm is hurting," they replied.

The four boys were gone by the first light of morning. We had spent the night talking about baseball and girlfriends, sharing photos but avoiding the war. Though I would never see them again, I felt as if these four young men had changed my life forever.

I met my wife, Marty Tracy, shortly after returning to the States from Vietnam. We moved to Maine several years later. By logging in the forest, heating with wood, drinking from Marty's pottery and wearing clothes made from the wool of our own animals, I tried to forget the past. Our first child, a daughter, Cora, was born in 1977.

One night in the winter of 1984, it was cold, very cold. The moon was full and filled my bedroom with a blue light. Trees cracked in the forest. High overhead in the heavens a small blinking red light made its way through the stars. For a moment the light seemed to hesitate, stopping to look at what it had dropped. Then the night turned to day with a blinding flash. I saw the side of my farmhouse nearest the blast burst into flames, the rooms of my children engulfed in a firestorm. Then came the screams of pain, of fear, of dying. I awoke, gripping my bedsheets, yelling for my wife and children.

As winter turned to spring, the nightmares gave way to a deep depression. It was 1984 and President Reagan was calling the Soviet Union the evil empire. The nuclear arms race was out of control. The local movie house was showing *Red Dawn*, in which high school students in rural America were mowed down by airborne attackers. Darth Vader had arrived and he was Russian. I would talk with my neighbors about what we could do to stop this madness. "What can one person do?" we would ask each other, agreeing that it was all beyond our control. Marty had just coordinated an international student gathering in our town that summer and her experience reminded me of my night on the Mekong. We decided I should take a trip to Russia.

"Mr. Hagerty, it is such a pleasure to meet you." Dressed in a pinstriped wool suit, Gucci shoes and an Italian silk tie, Nickolai Borisovitch Emelianov entered the door and extended a hand in greeting. He stood in contrast to the bare birch-paneled walls and the portrait of Lenin by the window. I had come to Moscow hoping to buy a small amount of Russian wool to blend with our Maine wool and, in the process, to make friends, if I could, with a Russian. With Emelianov's help I hoped to make knitting yarn and call it Peace Fleece. "With all due respect," Mr. Emelianov replied, "this idea of yours is a bit crazy. We all use the wool we grow to meet the needs of the Soviet people. We have never exported wool to America. Why should I sell wool to you?" At a loss for an explanation, I began to tell him my story, my history of the war and my wife and children in Maine. "If you and I don't do something today," I ended, "then the chance of my son or daughter growing up, falling in love, having a family of their own is greatly diminished." He turned from the window, saying, "You sound just like my wife." He then picked up his phone and made a call.

Five months later the first shipment of Soviet wool entered Boston Harbor and Peace Fleece was born. Peace Fleece, for me, has been a way to move beyond the pain of the 1960s, Vietnam and the Cold War. Our office is a sheep farm in Maine, a crowded family apartment in Moscow or the back of a pickup truck somewhere between Tel Aviv and Jericho. After we return from every trip, we appreciate the courage of our partners, many of whom are in the midst of political, social or economic crisis. Some are living in war zones. And we appreciate our own co-workers, neighbors and friends who make this part of America a wonderful place to raise a family and run a business.

By working with people who sell wool or tend to livestock every day, we hope to find a common ground that can slowly lead to mutual understanding and interdependence, no matter how deep the hurt or how old the conflict. We invite you to visit us here in Maine, on the Internet or through the pages of our catalogue.

Sheplova Village

Dalis Davidson

Landing at the Moscow airport in November, I find I'm excited and am not quite sure what to expect. My husband, Houston, and I are accompanying Peter Hagerty to Moscow to visit five sheep farms in the surrounding countryside. We will be escorted by Peace Fleece's Russian director, Luba

Reotova, who will be our driver and translator. I met Luba two years ago when she stayed at our farm in Maryland. In Moscow, Houston and I stay in her friend's apartment, three tiny rooms decorated with red rugs on the walls, Russian dolls and three TVs. After a good night's sleep, I look out of our 8th-story windows and see a winter wonderland. A few inches of snow have fallen during the night and left a beautiful white blanket. I like this first view of daylight, even though the sky is steel gray and the air looks very cold. A troop of Russian police walks by, eight in all, quite young-looking, small clouds escaping from their mouths. They wear long gray coats and fuzzy black hats—all very official. An old woman, hunched over, is sweeping the snow off the street out front with a loose handmade broom. I hear swoosh, swoosh, swoosh as the broom cleans wide swatches of snow off the pavement.

After a hearty breakfast, we leave Moscow for Pavel and Galina Potstrelov's farm in Sheplova, the first sheep farm on our tour. It's a three-hour drive. Luba whisks us through Moscow, honking at other drivers who cut her off or get too close (door handles nearly touching!). Finally we're out into the country; the roads get narrower and the villages farther apart. Night has fallen now, along with the temperature—the days are very short—and I wrap my arms around myself in the backseat and peer out the window. The villages are tiny now with small wooden houses, smoke curling from their chimneys and a single lightbulb yellowing the windows. We make the turn to Sheplova and go two miles down a snow-covered dead-end road. I see a twinkling of lights off in the distance. We hope Pavel and Galina are home, as they have no phone and don't know we're coming. Luba almost gets stuck in a ditch making a wrong turn into their drive. Yes, they're home. Dogs greet us as we get out, open the wooden gate and enter first one vestibule, then another. Finally we are standing in their warm log home.

After many greetings, hugs, kisses and introductions, we have tea and bread. A large Russian fireplace, the color of adobe, takes up one wall of the living area. I sit on the bench that's placed in front of the hot wall, put my back against it and am immediately comforted. Peter picks up a guitar that's hanging on the wall and plays and sings an impromptu song, Sheplova Blues. Pavel joins in, drumming on a homemade stool and yelling/singing his Russian version. We all start clapping and their dog howls and whines, making us all laugh. The night goes on, we're warm, fed and totally happy, beginning a new friendship with two Russian farmers. I couldn't imagine a better introduction to rural Russian life.

We start to get ready for bed. Luba and I put on coats, hats and mitts and Galina gives me her valenkis (felted wool boots that go up to my knees, and fortunately fit perfectly) and we race into the cold outside to the fence line to pee. The sky is star-strewn constellations, galaxies, the Milky Way, planets, all there for the viewing. It's so dark and crisp and silent. The ground is frozen hard with three inches of fresh, white snow. We squat in the dark, talking to each other in our own accents about the clarity of the evening, both inside and out. The men go to the back of the house where another wood stove is warming up the two sleeping rooms. The women get the toasty front room. Galina makes up the double bed for herself and Luba, and I take the smaller bed. Galina puts more wood on the stove. I hear it crackle and pop, and it makes me feel warm and cozy, especially since I'm snuggled under many heavy wool blankets. I drift off to sleep listening to my two Russian friends whisper in the dark.

I hear Galina up before dawn (which at this time of year is

8:00 A.M.) stoking the fire and preparing breakfast. I sit up in bed and see the most amazing red sunrise through the lace curtains. Outside, the landscape is white; I see weathered outbuildings, a big garden put to rest for the winter, a tiny steep-roofed outhouse, a wide flat field, the forest. Wrapping it all up is this fiery sunrise. I rush to get dressed, grab the camera and venture out to a farm greeting the new day.

I hear the rooster, coaxing everyone to wake up. The barn is a few steps through the fence gate. It's a low building with deep, overhanging eaves, made of logs with sisal chinking. Ducking through the doorway, I find many animals ready to greet me. The chickens are up, pecking around; Pavel's workhorse is patiently awaiting his breakfast, and the ducks are quacking to get out of their enclosure. The main part of the barn has a narrow center aisle with three lambing pens on the left and sections for veal cattle and a milk cow on the right. The Romanov sheep, a gray, woolly breed, able to withstand the brutal weather, are cozily housed on the left in three separate lambing pens. Three ewes have given birth to three sets of triplets and are being pampered in their pens. They have distinctive white markings on their face that make them look like tiny Holstein calves. Romanovs have two to four lambs twice a year—they're lambing machines! I immediately crawl over the gate to the last stall and fall in love with a two-week-old lamb with a white face and two large, black circles around her eyes. I pick her up and hold her close, nuzzling her and smelling her sweet lamb scent. She eventually baaahs for her mom, not sure of this human intrusion, and I gently put her down.

I'm called in for breakfast, which consists of bread, cheese, eggs, whey, butter, jam, tea and coffee. Everything we eat, except for the tea and coffee, was grown, raised or killed on the farm. After eating too much, we go out to work, following Pavel's lead. He hooks up his huge workhorse, a beautiful, bold animal with a mighty neck and gentle disposition. In his youth Pavel was a horse trainer and farrier in Moscow and his horses are very well managed. This horse wears a hand-hewn yoke, and hooked up to it is an old, weathered, flat wooden sled. The horse, with snorts of white breath bursting from his nostrils, pulls Pavel on the sled toward large round bales of hay stacked in the distant fields. We follow behind with pitchforks. The hay resembles giant frosted shredded wheat because the top layer is encrusted with 10 inches of snow and ice. Luba hacks away with an axe, cutting a line across the bale so we can peel away the outside. The horse moves the sled right in front of the bale and we heave, grunt, push and roll the bale onto the sled. We each stick our pitchfork into the sides, balancing it as the horse pulls the sled over the bumpy bits to the barn. The men unroll the bale, like a hay carpet, forking it into the barn while Luba and I jump on the stack as it gets higher and higher. We move five bales, then break for lunch.

Over lunch, the Potstrelovs and I discuss the possibility of my buying a lamb from them and keeping her on their farm—rather like an adoption. After many attempts at translating, Luba finally makes them understand the request. I want to help them out, so they will be able to continue to raise sheep and my little lamb will grow up and have more lambs and they'll benefit from my donation. I see a lot of head-nodding, so I get my purse and buy my first Russian Romanov lamb. We walk out and take many pictures of me with my little bundle of life.

That night at dinner I give out presents to our hosts. I'd brought along sheep vitamins, bungee cords and handmade soap, and while I was there, I knitted up a wool headband for each of them. They model the headbands, Pavel puts on his leather coat and shows off his new headpiece. I couldn't begin to repay them for what they'd given me—a warm welcome into their home, a look at how farmers a world away from our own farm in Barnesville, Maryland, can make a living and be happy, living off the land, being nearly self-sufficient, avoiding the rat race we call a life.

Leaving Pavel and Galina's the next day was very emotional for me. I really felt I'd bonded with them, even though I spoke no Russian and they spoke no English. Smiles and nods go a long way! I hugged Galina and couldn't let go. She talked to me the whole time and I'm sorry I couldn't understand a word of it. I'm hoping it was an invitation to visit again.

In Libya

Nan Browning, as told to Kathryn Gunn

My husband was appointed by the United Nations Food and Agricultural Organization to work in Libya in the 1960s. Since our children were grown up, I went with him. In order to see as much as I could of Libya, I went with my husband on many of his journeys to the more remote parts of the country. On one occasion we started out in the early morning. I was knitting away as we drove. We had gone a considerable distance when the truck we were traveling in broke down, not far from a fair-sized village. Fortunately we were traveling in convoy and were able to get help. We were towed into the village. Once we were there, one of the men saw me sitting and knitting away. He beckoned to me and indicated that I could enter one of the houses. Since it was growing very warm, I accepted the invitation and rolled up my knitting and put it on the truck seat. As I was walking toward the house he rushed back, picked up my knitting and handed it to me. I was rather surprised but accepted it and followed him inside the house. There I had one of the delightful surprises of my life. Inside a cool, immaculately clean room there were seven or eight women of about my own age—all knitting! I took the seat I was offered and took out my knitting. The women inspected my work closely and passed their own knitting over for me to look at. Almost all of them seemed to be knitting the most beautiful and intricately patterned multicolor socks. One woman showed me a new method of casting on for socks that I still use. We did not speak a word in common but I had one of the best mornings of my life.

Yungas Road

Jonna Gjevre

Bolivia is an increasingly modernized nation, but anyone traveling from La Paz to the semitropical paradise of Coroico must either fly or take the nearly medieval Yungas road. This one-lane dirt road occasionally widens to allow drivers to pass each other; but many of the passing points are decorated with white crosses and plastic flowers honoring the dead. Maria, who sat in the back of the van with her sister, mostly succeeded in ignoring these white crosses. She was absorbed in her knitting. She had survived the trip out to Coroico, and she would survive the trip back. Her guidebook and her sister Rose had warned her that the drive would be a white-knuckle affair, and it seemed to her that the best way to avoid panicking would be to knit.

Do not look out the window, Maria thought. Do not look. In the front seat, her brother-in-law Roberto periodically shouted encouraging words back to the two women, who tried not to notice that the narrow dusty road clung to the edge of cliffs that went down farther than they could see. The driver sat beside Roberto and (not encouragingly) crossed himself as he rounded each corner.

Maria had accompanied Rose and Roberto to Bolivia to hear them play Mozart's *Symphonie Concertante* with the COFES festival orchestra in Cochabamba. Rose and her husband were a violinist and violist, respectively, and had lived in Bolivia during the first year after their marriage. Maria was accompanying them to the festival this year, her trip paid for by the generous administrators at Marshall Field's, who awarded vacations to each of the computer programmers who had worked endless overtime through the Y2K crisis. Maria had chosen Bolivia, spending a tiny portion of her bonus on the luscious Missoni knitting kit that she'd brought along. The kit's space-dyed Brazza yarn and intricate saw-tooth intarsia pattern were classic Missoni design. Maria knew that most of the shabbily dressed systems analysts she worked with would never recognize or appreciate a Missoni sweater. But it wasn't for them, she thought; it was for her. She reveled in the detail, the luxury, and the authenticity of the design. She loved the idea of creating her own designer sweater with a series of precise yet simple stitches. Knitting in some ways was to her like writing code: the components were few and simple, but the patterns were endlessly complex. At times, she could imagine herself wearing the finished sweater to an elegant restaurant—the interlocking blue, purple, and charcoal tones contrasting with her long, pale blond hair. She would be mysteriously silent, but her sweater would whisper, "Look at me—clever, talented, cultured, refined."

The van pulled to a stop, and Maria looked up, expecting another excruciating series of back-and-forth maneuvers to pass an oncoming vehicle. But they were in an open spot with plenty of room to pass. And the vehicle in front of them was parked and empty. They got out of the van and walked over toward a group of men standing by the edge of the road. More white crosses, Maria noticed, as she took in the dry cream-colored rock walls across the valley. Directly behind her rose the sheer cliffs from which the road had been blasted and carved. To her right were the now-distant terraces of the Coroico coca plantations. Rose took Maria's arm and stopped, squinting in the sun. Roberto and the driver were speaking in low voices with the other men. "This is a guy thing," Rose told Maria. "We'd better wait by the van."

It was hot. They settled down in the shade of the van. Rose added more sunblock to her pale skin and pulled back her hair. Maria picked up her sweater and drew the live stitches toward the tips of her rosewood needles. Roberto walked over to them in a swirl of powdery white dust. "Ladies, we're going to stop here for a while," he said.

The men on the road were rescue workers and the partner of a driver who had gone over the edge the night before. The heavy fog had made it hard to see. The two truckers had stopped to park at the wide passing point and had piled stones behind the wheels to help keep the truck from slipping. The driver had climbed back into the truck to sleep, but his partner had stepped away to relieve himself. The rocks and the brakes did not hold, and the truck had plunged over the edge. Roberto could not even see the truck, it was so far down.

"Someone's rappelled down to the crash and attached ropes to the body," Roberto said. "I'm going to go help them pull it up." Maria settled into her knitting, marveling at Roberto's matter-of-fact tone. He was Bolivian and nothing surprised him, she considered—not the poverty, not the corruption, not even the dead bodies lying below the road. Rose had warned Maria not to bring American expectations and attitudes with her to South America, but how could she not?

Last week, she'd had her Doc Martens polished by one of the scruffy shoe boys on the square in Cochabamba. He charged her two bolivianos, which outraged Roberto, who said that the going rate in the small towns was one boliviano and in La Paz thirty cents. He questioned the boy, who gave him the lame excuse that he had taken extra time and polish to darken all of the heavy yellow stitching on the soles. How much was a boliviano worth? Twenty-five cents? She couldn't even remember. The next day, she had stood in the shadow of the cathedral while a different boy rubbed polish into Rose's embossed leather boots with his bare hands as he complimented Maria's soft corduroy pants. Roberto translated, "He's saying that your pants are the perfect fabric for polishing shoes—the fabric is so soft and plush." She tried to imagine herself admiring clothing not because it was stylish, but because it was suited for polishing shoes—because it would help her to earn a living, one boliviano at a time.

She looked up from her knitting. Roberto was in line with the other men, pulling on the rope. It's like a grisly tug-of-war, Maria thought, watching as the struggling men finally dragged the driver's body up to the roadside. The man's face and clothes were covered with powdery white dust, and his skin was drained of color. Yet his long black hair was blown about by the wind, dark strands of it floating and shimmering as if they still had life. Maria glanced at Rose, whose head was bowed as she made the sign of the cross. It seemed to Maria that she too should make some gesture, that she should in some way acknowledge what had happened. But she wasn't able to move. She could not speak, and her hands and arms were filled with luxurious, glittering yarn.

The Old Man's Cardigan

Kathryn Gunn

After I graduated from university, I went to do postgraduate work in London. As I made my way through the university grounds each morning I often saw an elderly man on a bicycle coming in the opposite direction. We would smile and nod at one another and gradually exchanged comments on the weather. One morning, however, he stopped and said, "Please excuse my asking. I cannot help noticing your knitted garments. Do you by any chance know how to knit?" I said that yes, I did, and had knitted these pieces myself. He hesitated for a moment and then he asked, "I wonder if you would do something for me. My late wife made a cardigan for me and I had a slight accident. It needs mending. I was wondering if you could. I have found some wool."

I did the job, which involved reknitting a cuff, and he thanked me very courteously. In the manner of casual encounters we did not exchange names, although he knew where I was working. We went back to talking about the weather. Months later a senior member of the university staff told me that he was one of the Law Lords, a member of the High Court in the United Kingdom. To me, however, he was always an old man on a bicycle who treasured a cardigan made by his wife.

The Road to Mwanza

Nicole Pritikin

I have traveled to many foreign countries and make it a point to never travel without my knitting. It doesn't matter what I bring with me; any kind of knitting will do. On this particular trip, I had brought a small shawl with not much of a pattern. It was to be a Christmas gift for my boyfriend's mother. I never thought that knitting would save my life, but on this trip, it saved both my life and my sanity.

In the summer of '95, I traveled to a remote village in Tanzania with a volunteer organization to study folklore, to see if I really wanted to pursue a degree in anthropology. The brochure said that accommodations would be primitive, which was fine; I've dealt with the hole-in-the-ground bathroom thing before. But from the start of this trip, everything seemed to go wrong. Our group leader, a professor from the U.S. and a native Tanzanian, abandoned us each day to go off on his own to collect oral histories, apparently needing us only for the money we provided. Our "hotel" had run out of water shortly after we arrived, which is a serious problem when the toilet is a drain in the floor of the bathroom that you flush with a dumped pail of water. Mosquitoes were eating us alive. We reeked from not bathing. By the fifth waterless day I had developed a bladder infection and a fever of 101 degrees.

After several days of washing my hands and body in a bucket of water with dead bugs floating on the surface and green slime on the edges, I knew there was no way I would cure a fever in these conditions and I was losing it. I went to several local "doctors," who believed that if you didn't have malaria, you weren't really sick. I knew I would never get better without being able to bathe, eat off clean plates, and get antibiotics, so I decided to leave. I'd take a bus to Mwanza, the nearest city, get treated, and then fly back early to Nairobi for some sightseeing.

Leaving was easier said than done. Buses came into this town but nobody knew when they would come again or if you would survive the trip, since the buses were usually packed five or six times beyond capacity and would tip over or break down regularly. As they went down the road, the buses would lean at a 45-degree angle with people hanging out of both sides. You could blow a puff of air in their direction and they would sway back and forth. Despite all better judgment, I bought a ticket for a bus to Mwanza. There was no schedule or any idea when the bus would come, so I sat down at the bus stop in the morning and waited. I pulled out the knitting and knit and waited and knit and waited and knit and waited. By mid-afternoon, word came around that my bus had broken down several hours away and would not be coming at all. Nobody knew when the next bus to Mwanza would be, or if there would be one at all.

Panic was setting in. I knew I had to get out of there; my bladder hurt and the fever was getting worse. I was in a foreign country completely alone, not able to speak more than five words of the language, and I was SICK. I did what any knitter would do: I sat and knit. I couldn't think of anything else to do—I couldn't decide whether to wait for another bus, or walk back to the "hotel" with its swampy bathwater. I knit and knit and knit. When I felt myself start to panic, I counted rows, I added yarn-overs, I knit two together, I made bobbles. After an hour of my knitting and contemplating my fate, an older woman approached me and pointed at my knitting. She talked in a language I didn't understand. I stopped knitting and displayed the pattern and my work so far. She smiled and kept babbling to me. Then she grabbed my arm and pulled (really hard too). She kept pulling. I didn't know what to do.

I finally decided there was no point in fighting with her so I got up, took my knitting and all my other stuff, and let her lead me away from the bus stop to God-knows-where. She kept smiling and chatting in Swahili as she led me down one dark alley after another. We finally got to a little shack where a young man was standing. He told me (in broken English) that his cousin drove a cab and could drive me to Mwanza since the bus was not coming anytime soon. The woman just smiled at him and then at me. The idea of getting in a car with people I did not know didn't sit well, but my other option was waiting for an undetermined amount of time for a bus that might or might not come, and if it did, might or might not break down. I checked out the car, an old Peugeot from the 1960s or '70s; it seemed old but fine. Who was I to complain anyway? So we worked out the details, and off I went, panic still not far away.

The driver and his "navigator" were two young boys who could not have been more than thirteen years old. That was not the only problem, however. I didn't figure out the real trouble I was in until we were already about a half an hour out of town: neither boy spoke English and it seemed that neither knew where we were going. I had picked up a few words of

Swahili, but none of them related to driving. I kept asking them, *"Gina lango nani?"* (What is your name?), but my accent or pronunciation must have been off because all they did was laugh. Communication was impossible.

Again, I turned to knitting. I sat quietly in the backseat knitting, trying to concentrate on the complicated pattern I had now created. Knit one, purl three, yarn over, knit two, purl three . . . Despite all my efforts to concentrate on my knitting and not panic, a bad feeling settled into my stomach after about an hour out of town, when the boys started yelling in Swahili at each other. They kept pointing in different directions and talking rapidly. Neither one knew where to go. I asked, "Mwanza?" and pointed straight ahead. Each boy turned around, said "Mwanza!" and pointed in a different direction. This wasn't the kind of road where you could just pull over and ask someone for directions, either. In the hour we had been driving, we had passed next to nothing. No stores or towns, just bushes and scraggly trees with an occasional hut in the distance. Every so often, the dirt tracks we had been following would suddenly fork and the boys would argue again.

Knit one, purl three, yarn over, knit two, purl three . . . I was convinced I would never get to Mwanza. I knit to ignore the rattling of the car and the arguing of the boys. I knit to stave away the panic. I knit to ignore the fact the we weren't on what anyone would consider a road, just a set of dirt tracks that would begin and end without warning. I knit and knit and knit. I knit so I wouldn't have to look up and see that we were in what looked like the middle of nowhere, or at least what looked like the same part of the road we had passed three hours ago. As I knit, horrible thoughts crossed my mind. What if these boys tried to hurt me? What would I do? There was nobody around for miles. What if they weren't headed for Mwanza at all but some other place where nobody spoke English and I wouldn't be able to get back? What if we ran out of gas? Several hours had gone by. I had no idea where we were or if we were headed even remotely in the right direction. I did the only thing I could: I knit.

Just when I figured things couldn't get any worse, I heard a loud clanking noise from the back of the car. Clank, clank, clank, clank. The boys stopped in the middle of nowhere, walked calmly around the car and down the dirt tracks a little ways, picked up the car's muffler, opened the rear car door, set the muffler down gently next to me on the backseat, and drove off. Now, I don't know much about cars but I figured the muffler is there for a reason and it probably isn't a good thing if it comes off completely. The boys didn't seem fazed by the loss and just continued on. I knit on and tried to be like the boys and not let the muffler's loss bother me.

After four hours, I had given up hope of ever seeing Mwanza, let alone a bathroom or people who spoke English. The sun was setting but looking out toward the horizon, I could see the lights of a city. "Mwanza, Mwanza, Mwanza?" I shouted, bouncing up and down and pointing. "Mwanza," they said, looking back, as if they knew it would be there all along. And who knows? Maybe they did.

That night, I stayed at a hotel where little antlike flying bugs invaded every crevice of my luggage and feasted on my arms and legs. I didn't care, I was alive and in Mwanza. I pulled the knitting out of my bag. It was gorgeous, the shawl to end all shawls, with the most beautiful lace design ever. I'll be honest though, I never gave away the shawl as a gift and I never use it myself, except to inspire nightmares. It rests on a shelf in my closet and reminds me of Africa, a broken-down car, dirt roads, and swampy bathwater.

part three

family and special folk

Grandmothers

The Eisenhower Jacket

Marisa Labozzetta

My Mary Janes barely tapped the sidewalk as I tried to keep up with Mamma's fast pace. My left shoulder ached from the upward stretch my arm maintained while Mamma, taking giant strides, pulled me along the crowded avenue. Familiar landmarks whizzed by: Amato's Bakery; the Walker Theater; the redbrick house with white pillars that belonged to Dr. Bonamassa; the vegetable stand where grumpy old Mr. Marchese stopped customers from dipping into his precious bushels of produce and filled their paper bags himself. "Move, Marisa. Grandma's waiting to take you to Henny's."

Grandma was always waiting for us: sitting on her front

porch, tapping her black orthopedic shoe, exclaiming loud enough for the neighbors to hear that we were late for whatever—christenings, holidays, Sunday dinner. Even when we were least expected, Grandma greeted us with a disapproving look that said our surprise visit was well overdue. Grandma was Mamma's mother-in-law, which only heightened my mother's anxiety to arrive on time. "Aren't you excited?" Mamma asked, her high heels extending farther and farther away from her body with each step. That Grandma was going to knit me another outfit didn't excite me at all. Rather it had filled my stomach with enough queasiness to make me throw up my morning eggnog.

I hadn't always hated my grandmother's knitting projects. I once relished holding skeins of yarns on my hands as a cousin sat across from me and rolled the woolen string into a big fat ball that would be easier for Grandma to work with. I had enjoyed the trips to Henny's Yarn Shop where a machine with two sticks replaced human hands, and colorful skeins automatically became cushiony spheres. There, knitting needles of every length and width and whole rainbows of yarn lined the walls. There, chatty women congregated, eager to make something wonderful out of nothing. There, with a pair of short needles and leftover wool, Grandma taught me how to make Barbie doll blankets and scarves.

Where Grandma learned to knit—Italy or America—I never discovered. She just seemed to know how to work strands of wool into marvelous textiles, as though it were a special gift that God had endowed her nimble fingers with. She knitted while watching television, never glancing down at the threads that were becoming a Perry Como sweater with a zipper up the front for my father, or a dress with shimmering gold leaves across the bosom for my mother. The adults used to say that Grandma could knit in a movie theater: meaning that she could knit in the dark without dropping a stitch or referring to any instructions. In fact, Grandma couldn't read. I often sat at the beige and white Formica table with her and Aunt Sadie while Sadie translated the directions not only into Italian but into a simple language—the knitting equivalent of a pinch of this and a handful of that—at which Grandma nodded with recognition. I had adored my hunter green and peach jumper, my navy cable stitch sweater, and my purple mittens with white stars. The berets always posed a problem, however, since wire put in them to retain their shapes tended to find its way out of the hats and, on occasion, into my face, threatening my eyes.

I had loved Grandma's knitting, until the day she announced that she was making me an Eisenhower jacket. It was this cropped military-style jacket, a version of the one our current President Eisenhower had worn during World War II, that turned me sour on knitting.

Grandma and I had entered Henny's Knit Shop as we had so many other times. The clickety-clack of knitting needles reverberated through the narrow, deep store as the attractive and revered Henny went from woman to woman, advising them on this stitch or that. The ball-making machine whirred; woolen globes swelled like magic. On graph paper, Henny reproduced designs that the women showed her, filling tiny squares with X's so that the women would be able to re-create the patterns with yarn.

Grandma selected the wool for the Eisenhower jacket. The yarn she chose was thick; the jacket would be heavy and warm. And it was *brown*. Even as a six-year-old, I had a budding fashion sense. Brown was—well, boring. As boring as a pair of Grandpa's shoes, or my father's wallet, or my mother's handbag. Besides, it blended in with my chestnut hair and eyes and olive skin. With a pair of brown leggings and the jacket's matching cap that my mother would dress me in, I would feel like a clump of dirt from my grandfather's vegetable garden.

Then came the disgrace: How much wool would the jacket need? Henny made me stand up on a stool and, like a model being prepared for the runway, measured me from head to toe. Now the creation of this garment had collided with a certain characteristic of mine: I had a very small appetite and, in an Italian family, this was equal to a chronic affliction—a monumental handicap. While my cousins played outside after dinner, I often sat alone, confined to Grandma's kitchen table, my cold steak coated with white waxy fat, my milk on the verge of curdling.

Grandma, unable to suppress her embarrassment at having such an emaciated offspring, sought the commiseration of strangers. "*Guardate come* skeeeny!" she bellowed, inviting all of the women to take a look at her deformed granddaughter. The blood seemed to drain from my body. Where it went, I never knew, but I became so dizzy that I fell off of the stool and sailed for what seemed like eternity—all eyes upon me, mouths aghast—onto the cold linoleum floor.

The experience at Henny's Knit Shop wasn't the end to my humiliation. While I rode around in circles on my tricycle in front of my apartment house one afternoon, a fragile old lady—her paper bag of groceries firmly in hand—gingerly stepped around me, so as not to be run over. "Careful, little boy," she said. That was it! Not only was the jacket ugly, it had been made in imitation of something a man had worn and therefore changed my gender to boot.

I couldn't articulate my feelings at the time. I simply refused to wear the jacket. My refusal to wear such a well-crafted garment ever again became a source of utter aggravation to my mother, who tried to convince a suspicious Grandma that I had undergone a sudden and significant growth spurt.

Arthritis and old age eventually surfaced in my grandmother's art. In college, I asked her to knit me a pullover. I bought the bright raspberry wool at a shop in Boston, where I attended school. Grandma made the sweater, but it was filled with imperfections. I wore the sweater. I have never thrown it out.

This past summer my nineteen-year-old daughter, born the same week my grandmother passed away, expressed interest in learning how to knit. Straining my memory, I showed her how to cast on, to knit and purl; it was all I knew. Before long, she was producing multicolored hats and mittens with intricate patterns. She is making me a periwinkle cardigan for Christmas. She knits in between university classes, on bus rides home, while watching TV. She knits with the speed and precision of years of experience. It is in her blood: I know it.

Dancing with Grandma

Elliott Kronenfeld

I was once told that being with someone during the last moments of life was a terrific honor. My grandmother Anna gave me that special honor—one that would change the rest of my life. Anna was an amazing woman. At 93, she had already outlived her husband and all of her children. We truly believed that she was going to outlive us all. She still worked a full-time job and ran circles around the rest of us. In September 1993, I got a call from her asking me to go to the doctor's office with her. I knew this was not good news, because her independent nature would only allow her to call for help if she had no other choices. The doctor confirmed the bad news: pancreatic cancer. Not a good thing. It's a fast-moving cancer. She had six weeks to six months, max.

My sister, Melissa, did not take the news well. She had just got engaged and was planning for a November wedding more than a year away. She flatly refused to change her date. Saying firmly, "My grandmother will be at my wedding," she displayed the fiery determination she had for most things. I tried to explain that there was no way. If she wanted Grandma there, she would simply have to move the date up. It was like talking to a stone. As the weeks went on, I called Melissa to tell her that things were not looking good. Grandma tired easily. She lost her appetite. Didn't want visitors. Couldn't do her own chores anymore. Again, I strongly suggested she move her wedding date. Again, my suggestion fell on deaf ears. The wedding came and Grandma and I got on a plane and flew from Boston to Florida. Even though it was not her choice, Grandma allowed me to put her in a wheelchair. Grandma was a real trouper. She weathered a hurricane, the wheelchair and the wedding with grace and style. She was exhausted.

I was ready to take Grandma back to Mom's house, when she told me she wanted to dance one dance. I scooped her up in my arms and started to sway with the music. I was painfully aware of how much weight she had lost as she gripped tightly and kissed my face all over. When the music ended, I told her it was time to go. After one parting moment of a sweet old woman and beautiful bride in white, we left. My sister got her wish. The next morning we had to take an emergency medical flight home.

Grandma started to deteriorate quickly after that. She became completely bedridden. She knew she was dying. We told her that she could spend her last days in any fashion she desired. To my surprise, she told me that she did not want to leave her yarn stash behind. We would have to knit it up. So, with my 93-year-old bedridden dying grandmother, I learned how to cast on. We started with simple knit and purl stitches. She taught me how to fix my mistakes and how to rip it all out and start again. It was frustrating because my nimble healthy hands couldn't keep up with her arthritic weak ones.

As she would move my fingers around the skein, pulling with just the right tension, we would talk. We talked about her life and what it meant. "Grandma, you have lived almost a century. Here is what that means to me: the Roosevelts, the Kennedys, World War I, World War II, Korea, Vietnam, the Gulf War. The invention of the television, airplane, computer, and fax machine. The global economy, rights for blacks, women, and gays. Pretty amazing stuff. So, out of all the experiences you have had in your life, what is the most amazing moment?" Without missing a beat, she responded, "The day I married my husband." I was stunned. She was not your typical beauty and had married late in life. My grandfather had died when my father was a young boy. She never remarried. They didn't have many years together and I never knew him. She had carried a torch for him all these forty-five years later.

As we progressed to simple patterns and yarn-overs, Grandma declined more. I had to call the hospice in. "Grandma, you know the end is near. What does it feel like and what do you think is going to happen?" "It doesn't hurt at all," she answered. "I am just tired. I am going to see my family. Your father. I am going to tell them all about you and your brother and sister. Tell them everything." She silently fell asleep again. I found myself continuing with the pattern she was working on. Not thinking really, but just needing to do something with my hands.

The next day we picked up our knitting again. "I can't believe you made it to Melissa's wedding. You really surprised me—but then again, you always did. You have always had a special relationship with her. She was the only grandchild whose birth you witnessed. What did you think when you saw her for the first time?" "I was incredibly sad," she said. "I wanted your grandfather to know her. He would have loved her and been so good to her. I vowed that day to live long enough to dance one dance at her wedding to represent your grandfather. We always talked about dancing at our grandchildren's weddings." As she slowly started to bind off the end of our project, I realized in great clarity what the past months had meant. She didn't dance with me. All those years later, she was dancing with a man I never knew. I wanted to ask her more, but she had fallen asleep again. I left our newly completed afghan—made by a dying woman and a grandson who had so many questions—across her tiny body.

After staring at her for quite a long time, I picked up the needles myself and cast on again. When she woke up I was going to show her all that I had learned. I took the afghan into the living room and studied the work and tried to replicate it. I was never able to show her my work. She died the next morning and took with her the stories of a lifetime. After they came and took her away, I walked home to my house with my worsted-weight afghan in my hand. Truly it is one of my most prized possessions. Now as I knit complicated cables and Norwegians, I think of two people: the person I am knitting the project for and my grandmother—for all the gifts she had given me.

A Twist in the Yarn

Zoë Blacksin

The needles sigh and crackle under Grandmother's glowing eye as I watch her knit the autumn into winter. The room is still and silent except for the fluttering of her parchment hands over the dull silver of the needles, the hushing of the wool as it's pulled out of the skein and into the sweater, a metamorphosis. Grandmother smiles at me with matzo-ball eyes and pulls me closer into her babushka embrace. *Watch, my darling, it's so easy. Just twisting and knotting, you'll pick it up in no time.*

As I twist the yarn around my fingers, Grandmother twists me into the stories she loves to tell about our family. As I learn to feel the rhythm in the stitches, her words flow with the current of her hands. She tells me how our men tilled the dark earth in Romania while the women spun and knit for dark Romanian queens. The wives and the mothers of our family kept the patterns in their hands and knit in the darkness to save the candlelight for the men, who pored over siddurs in the evenings, rocking back and forth like the candle flames themselves. Hands were greasy with lanolin and needles chirped and chuckled the babies to sleep.

Grandmother whispers to me as we start off with scarves and dollhouse rugs. *All the women have the patterns in their hands. You have the skill under your fingers and you don't know it yet. Just let them go—they will begin to remember.* I continue on to hats and socks, then mittens and gloves. Suddenly I'm knitting with nine different skeins of wool at once. I knit in cables and ribs, my stitches become smaller and increasingly intricate. *Twist the knots into stitches and bind the stitches into rows.* Grandmother sings over the flurry of my fingers. *God knows how long it's been done this way. My mother would whisper prayers into her wool as she knit, and you never got cold in one of her sweaters*, Baruch Hashem.

Soon, I can't put my needles down. I smuggle my knitting into biology lectures and spend all my money purchasing new patterns and more wool. I love the feel of the bamboo needles as they tap out a song under my hands, and the utter satisfaction of wearing items I make keeps me warmer than the wool itself. The anger and frustrations that I bring home at the end of the day, attached to my body like burrs, find their way out through my hands into the wool, and are stitched into beautiful things rather than festering in the back of my mind.

I knit in the darkness before sleep, guided by the wool twisted around my fingers, letting them follow the pattern they seem to know by themselves. Unwittingly, I have twisted myself into a knot and knotted myself into another row of our family. In the darkness I can feel the women surrounding me, dropping holy words into the wool like honey as we knit together. The rhythms of our hands harmonize. I cannot tell the cracklings of my needles from theirs. Let the men have the precious candlelight, we don't need it. We have knit ourselves together, safe in the darkness, and nothing disturbs the silence but the hush of the morphing wool, and the soft sound of our needles, sighing.

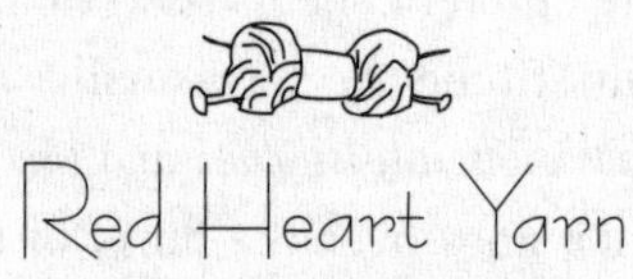

Red Heart Yarn

Zaina Keller Flickinger

When I was ten years old, I visited my grandparents on their farm in Kentucky. It was the first time that I'd been away from home without my parents or my two older brothers. But I was ready for an adventure. My grandmother was a very wise woman; she knew that her city-bred granddaughter might need some kind of entertainment other than looking at the tobacco fields and visiting the henhouse. When she asked me if I would like to learn to knit, I said I would, although I wasn't really sure at the time. It was the polite thing to say. Grandmother took me to the nearby town and encouraged me to select my own yarn and needles, and then brought me home for my first lesson. I had chosen a variegated Red Heart yarn—yarn was all 100 percent wool in those days. Grandmother praised my choice; she said I would be able to see every stitch as I knitted. She showed me a simple cast-on method that I now recognize as a backward loop cast on. The knit stitch was next. I decided that this was indeed going to be fun.

We started a practice piece, but soon it was time to start supper. My grandmother was a wonderful cook. She knew just how to feed the fire in her big wood-burning stove, with the hot-water reservoir at the side. She could test the temperature of the oven by putting her hand in, knowing when it was hot enough to turn biscuits and cornbread a fine golden-brown.

After supper, we picked up our knitting once again, but after a time, she said we had knitted enough for one day and would knit some more tomorrow. My piece had many holes and funny-looking stitches—in fact, I had MORE stitches than when I first started! Grandmother told me not to worry. The knitting just needed to relax, she said; by morning it would look much better. And she was right. The next morning, my knitting was smooth and pretty, just like Grandmother's. This went on for several days, until it was time for me to go home. By then, I'd knitted a rectangular piece that Grandmother sewed together to make a little clutch purse. She fashioned a loop and sewed on a button to make a closure. I was very proud of my little purse and carried it to school every day that next year.

Over fifty years—more than fifty now!—I have knitted many things: sweaters, scarves, socks, mittens, a purse or two. Knitting has led me to many friendships that I treasure and has given me hours of pleasure. But my very favorite memory of knitting is how my very wise grandmother encouraged me by praising my choice of yarn and then convincing me that the knitting "relaxed" all by itself during the night. I can picture in my mind how she must have smiled as she fixed those holes and eliminated the extra stitches after I went to bed. What a treasure that will always be for me!

Stitched with Love

Erica Orloff

Some people can make you feel as if you are the only person in the whole wide world. My grandmother Irene was that kind of person. She had six grandchildren, and I feel I was her favorite—and I'm sure that every one of her grandchildren felt that she loved them best. When I was a child, each talk with her made me feel as though she had been waiting breathlessly, in some state of suspended animation, for me—just me—to come along and tell her: that I'd seen fairies amongst the lilies of the valley or a ghost at the abandoned house down the road, or that I wanted to be a writer when I grew up. I would capture ladybugs and lightning bugs and dandelions. She accepted weeds as if they were roses and ladybugs as if they were rare jewels. Feelings like that are intangible. They run through you, are part of you, but you can't hold them in your hand or caress them against your cheek.

The wisdom and confidence that my grandmother imparted were gifts enough, but luckily for me and all her grandchildren, she also left a tangible reminder of her love in the afghans she knitted. Each grandchild could pick the colors for his or her afghan. My sister Stacey wanted hot pink and purple and, despite the fact I am sure knitting this made Grandma cringe, hot pink and purple she got. Michael and Robert got afghans, just as the girls did. The afghans kept us warm all winter at home, and were dragged off to dorm rooms to comfort cases of homesickness. The stitches were beautiful and intricate. There was nothing like hearing the click-click-clack of her knitting needles, knowing the hours of work and energy going toward your very own afghan. We made the important decisions together: Did I want fringe? And if so, what kind? Knotted? Did I want a lacy stitch or something that looked more solid? These were serious issues. After all, your afghan would last forever.

As she got older, she confessed to me that she could no longer do such intricate afghans. I remember visiting her one Sunday and her saying, "I just had to rip out every darn stitch because my eyes aren't what they used to be." Even when I told her an error wasn't noticeable, she would never tolerate mistakes. Her afghans had to be perfect.

By the time my daughter was born, Grandma was truly getting up there in years, and she had endured open-heart surgery. All during my pregnancy, I prayed fervently that she would live to see her first great-grandchild. We wrote to each other often, and she kept reminding me to "tell that great-grandchild of mine to hurry up so we can have one more baby to love in this family."

I named my daughter Alexa Irene, and I made plans to visit New York to have her baptized in the church my grandmother attended. When I arrived, my grandmother presented me with a box. I opened it and pulled out a bright yellow miniature afghan, just right for an infant. Grandma was a little critical. "Over here I missed a stitch somewhere. It's a little crooked. But every stitch was stitched with love." Through tears I thanked her. Who noticed the imperfections? The love itself was perfect.

The blanket has now survived three children, though my grandmother has passed away. Every night, I tiptoe into my youngest's bedroom. After she is asleep, I wrap her carefully in the yellow afghan. She's three, and it's almost too small for her, but I want her to feel the strength and love in that blanket. I tuck it up under her chin, and whisper, "Every stitch was stitched with love." And sometimes, I can almost hear a heavenly click-click-clack of knitting needles.

Grandmothers Are Supposed to Sit and Knit

Christine Rusch

(*for Jonathan*)

I wanted so much to fit in, but I never did. Other kids were after the most popular clothes and the coolest dates. I was looking for the secret of life, even back in second grade, in the days when I spent my lunch hours with my dad's mother.

She lived in an old house with a rambling porch a couple of blocks from the school, while my parents had built their dream home in the hills far from town. If you sat on the front porch you could hear her practicing her chords. She was a teacher of voice and piano. She had been raised on a Pennsylvania farm, the only girl of thirteen children, the one who baked forty loaves of bread and twenty pies a week, cleaned all the chamber pots and worked the garden, and was glad when it rained so she could sew. Late at night, exhausted, she would go to the piano and practice.

An overworked and abused young woman with deep blue eyes, she caught something she called a "social disease" from the man her daddy made her marry. When the doctor told her she would die unless she had all her female organs taken out, she informed him she would just as soon die. She ran away to New York City and stole my grandfather from his common-law wife and children. She made the headlines as The Singing Mother, raising four boys while giving recitals at

Town Hall and making life hell for every woman who tried to "steal" the boys away from her. Later in life she refused to be called Grandmother, so I called her Nanny. Nanny had a wash and set and manicure every Saturday morning, no matter what. She liked her Campbell's chicken noodle soup with chopped hard-boiled egg, but I preferred mine plain. All through those long-ago lunches, she used to tell me about how good she was, how hard she worked, how beautifully she sang, and how men had only one thing on their minds.

My mother's Mamusz ran away, too, from German-occupied Poland to Milwaukee, where she and Djadja struggled to raise their four little girls, never for a moment forgetting the baby who was buried in Poland or the little boy who was stillborn after two endless days and nights of hoping in the upstairs of a duplex on the South Side. Mamusz was the best cook in Milwaukee, and when there was no money for groceries and nothing in the cupboard except a little flour, she would serve flour-and-water soup, and weep. The earliest memory I have is visiting her grave, when I was three. There were forty-eight cars at her funeral.

It used to annoy me, that neither of my grandmothers matched the ones in the stories or in the movies. I was embarrassed, as though somehow it was my fault that, out of all the kids in school, I was the only one whose grandmothers didn't bake me cookies and knit me sweaters. One day in second grade I was standing in the lavatory line when the girl behind me tapped me on my shoulder.

"You going to your grandmother's for lunch?"

"Yes," I said. "I do every day." It felt good to say that there was something that happened every day, something I could count on besides my parents' fighting.

"Where does she live?"

"It's a long walk," I said. "She and my grandfather have a little house in the woods."

"What woods?" the girl asked.

"You can't see it from here," I said. "My grandfather builds little wooden dolls, and my grandmother knits little clothes for them."

I didn't see this statement as a lie. I saw it as a way of honoring how life should be. Sometimes you want something so much that you make it that way.

When I ran away and eloped and moved far from everyone, I thought everything would be different. At last things could be the way they were supposed to be; I set out to make them that way. I searched recipe books and cooked warm, flavorful chapati—Indian flatbreads—from nothing but flour and water. I baked bread and made pies. I learned how to crochet and how to knit, and how to tell the difference. Knitting uses two needles, and if you make a mistake, you've ruined the whole piece, and you have to start over. But crocheting is different. When you crochet, you use just one little hook, and if you make an error, all you have to rip out is your mistake, and then proceed. As nearly as I can tell, the secret of life is to crochet instead of knit. The difference between flour-and-water soup and chapati is the difference between giving up and working at it, looping and pulling, looping and pulling, trusting that every stitch will make a difference.

"You Have to Make Something"

Connie Elizabeth Tintinalli

About 35 years ago, my grandmother patiently taught me, her preschooler granddaughter, how to knit. My first project was a red wool scarf. It was rather short (but then, so was I!), as I was anxious to call it finished. There are actually only two stitches in knitting—the knit stitch and the purl stitch. All patterns of varying degrees of complexity and endless variety are simply combinations of these two stitches—a series of knots precisely formed to create a fabric that can be as delicate and airy as lace or heavy and dense as a fisherman's sweater. My next endeavor was a rather complicated (but still diminutive) white hat with a cable stitch that stretched from ear to ear and tied beneath the chin. I proudly wore that hat through many winters, until my ears grew too far apart. My projects increased in complexity and ambition as I grew into adolescence—sweaters for myself, my family, and, in my 20s, for a lover (quite a risky undertaking: Will it be finished before the relationship ends?). When a sweater I began for my soon-to-be-born nephew was finished after he had outgrown it and was suitable to be worn only by his teddy bear, I accepted that my life was too frantic and busy to allow for the gentle relaxation of tying wool into knots.

Some 10 years passed with my knitting bag inhabited by a (potential) sweater, with only a back and half of a front. Walking on Toronto's Bayview Avenue one day early in January 1996, I was strangely compelled to enter a knitting store, drawn by some inexplicable force. I fell in love with some hand-dyed yarn—yarn that began sapphire blue and wandered into azure and magenta and finally a midnight purple, bringing to mind the colors that saturate the sky as night falls, colors with the evanescent quality of a dragonfly's wings.

"Don't be silly," I told myself, "you never have time to knit anymore." I left the store and continued to do my errands. But on my way home, I was drawn back to the shop. I bought the yarn and a pattern, telling myself that, if nothing else, the yarn itself was so beautiful it was worth possessing if only to look at now and again.

The next day, my grandmother entered the hospital and was diagnosed with a heart ailment. I took up the enchanting yarn and began to knit. I think I believed that each stitch could somehow bind her closer to me, to the earth, to life. She recovered and, with medication, continued to embrace life and experience, with as much energy and determination as she had before. I was torn between finishing the sweater or leaving it unfinished, just in case I needed another miracle. I took up the sweater again a year later, waiting anxiously in the corridor of a London hospital with my mother while my father underwent heart surgery. Knit—inhale. Purl—exhale. Knit—inhale. Purl . . . With his complete recovery, I set the magical sweater aside. The following summer, my grandmother slipped and fell, hitting her head on the porch steps, and we lost her hours later to a brain hemorrhage. I was sleeping, unaware of her accident, when I should have been knitting. Heartbroken, the yarn no longer mystical, I finally completed the sweater. I finished it off with antique silver buttons, treasures that I found in her battered old button tin.

I have started to worry whenever I feel the urge to knit. I

had hoped last September that my compulsion to begin again came from the impending change of seasons, an anticipation of the coming autumn winds. But I fear that no one, certainly not I, could have fashioned a knot strong enough to keep my dear friend Richard from leaving this earth.

I have my grandmother's knitting guides now, a collection published in series, which she carefully assembled in two small brown binders. The list of abbreviations and translations has come to fascinate me. They seem to me to speak not of the stitches that comprise the garment, but of the fragments that make up a life. I pick through the English abbreviations: beg—beginning; rem—remaining; cont—continue; foll—following; sl—slip; tog—together. But there are also Italian terms: *ancora*—again; *totale*—complete; *volta*—time; *passare*—to pass; *tutti*—all; *senza*—without; *ultimo*—last. And then there are the French terms: *changement*—change; *terminer*—end; *laisser*—leave. I imagine composing the story of a life based on these terms.

As all knitted garments are created by the endless combinations of only two stitches, my grandmother's unconditional love also taught me that life is composed of love and hope: a series of knots precisely formed, ties that form relationships and experiences that bind us together. Her passing left a hole in my life the way a dropped stitch or pulled thread can unravel a work (or a dream). But while she has slipped from my grasp, she continues and remains complete within my heart.

Whenever I begin to feel entangled and trapped in necessary tasks, I hear my grandmother's voice telling me that *her* mother used to admonish her: "You have to make something, Sarah Elizabeth. You shouldn't spend all your time cooking and cleaning—those things are never done. You have to make something!" And make things she did—slippers, sweaters, dresses, rugs, doilies, afghans, doll clothes, a house full of love. Her words still resound in my head, although recently the text has changed slightly, but the voice is the same. "You have to make something, Connie Elizabeth! You have to make something."

The Reluctant Child

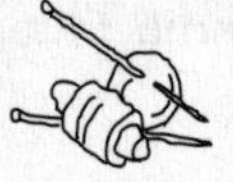

The Afghan

Edward Bear

It was wartime: World War II. We lived in Southern California at the time. My father was an Air Raid Warden, nightly making the rounds to be sure everyone had their blackout curtains up. Serious business. My brother was in the Navy, somewhere up near the Aleutian Islands on a minesweeper, although I don't think we knew at the time where he really was. There were all those posters staring out at you from grocery store and post office walls. Uncle Sam with his index finger to his lips: A SLIP OF THE LIP CAN SINK A SHIP. Constant reminders. So if we knew where he was, we never told; I'm sure of that.

I don't actually remember how I learned to knit. As I think

back, it must have been my mother who taught me, because I don't recall anyone else in the family knitting; there was only my sister, a year older, and my brother, seven years my senior and off to war. My father, in all likelihood, would rather have faced a firing squad then be caught with a knitting needle in his hand.

In my memory my mother was always cooking, or reading one of the many mystery books she got from the library (my mother got the allotted ten a week nearly every week—she probably read the same ones over and over again), or knitting or crocheting shawls, doilies, headrests, and the like. At some point, before I became aware that "real boys don't knit," I must have asked her to teach me. So I learned. And I enjoyed it. I don't recall telling anyone. I'm sure it was my evil sister who informed certain people at Chatsworth Park Grammar School that I could knit. She must have, because when the Red Cross came to the school to ask for volunteers to knit an afghan for "our boys overseas," my teacher (the beloved, if sometimes cranky, Mrs. Gore), confronted me. Somehow, she knew I could knit, and she wanted me to join the group that was going to knit an afghan for one of our boys overseas. Our poor, cold boys overseas. Mrs. Gore could be very persuasive. My mother thought it was a grand idea. She was in love with grand ideas. But how could I refuse? My very own brother was one of the boys overseas. He too was cold perhaps.

Of course I should have known that everyone else in the knitting circle was female. I didn't—but I should have. There were nine of them. Nine girls—and me. If there were other boys who could knit, they were smart enough not to tell anyone. I was eleven or twelve years old at the time, still too young to think that girls were anything but useless members of the human race, most of them involved in a conspiracy to make my life even more difficult than it was. My sister was a prime example. Of course she lied when I accused her of telling Mrs. Gore that I could knit. There wasn't much I could do directly, because she could still beat me up if it came to that. I was gaining ground, but she was still bigger and tougher. So I squealed on her to my mother, who somehow failed to grasp the gravity of the situation. She brushed aside the obvious betrayal by her treacherous daughter and suggested that I "give it a try." My mother was always big on giving things a try. That and grand ideas.

So there I was, probably in the sixth or seventh grade, spending recess time knitting an afghan for our boys overseas. It was bad enough that I had to do it in the first place, but then to have to give up recess, too . . . A small enough sacrifice, said Mrs. Gore, considering what our boys are doing for us. I, who was one of the best dodgeball players in the entire school, was knitting an afghan while my friends were out playing dodgeball. I began to hate the war.

And the worst was yet to come.

When the afghan was finally completed (it took only a few weeks, though it felt like months) I was asked to make the presentation to the Red Cross representatives in front of the whole school. I'm sure Mrs. Gore thought it would be a nice touch to have a boy, the only boy in school who could knit, make the presentation. An oddity of sorts. I, Mr. Dodgeball himself, was going to have to stand up in front of the entire school (there were actually less than a hundred of us), make a speech, and present this afghan to the Red Cross representatives. Mrs. Gore wrote the speech for me and I tried to memorize it. It was then that I discovered another interesting fact: I couldn't (and still can't) memorize things. Luckily I never wanted to be an actor. After repeated assurances that, if I just put my mind to it, I could, and my vehement protests that I couldn't, they finally gave in and allowed me to read the prepared text. When Doomsday arrived, there I was standing in front of the entire school in the auditorium getting ready to read from two small three-by-five cards. Useless Sally Mayfield and Doris Green held up the patchwork afghan for all to see. Even some parents came. Of course my mother was there, basking in the glow of my first (and I hoped last) public appearance. My father wisely had other things to do. For some reason Mr. McElvain, the owner of McElvain's Market, was there, though I'm not sure why. It was widely rumored that he had a serious drinking problem. Maybe he didn't have anything else to do that day.

The presentation was mercifully short. I said something about how we all pitched in, willingly gave up our recess time (ha!), and each knitted four one-foot-by-one-foot squares (notice the different colors?—applause). Mrs. Eudora Mayfield (Useless Sally's mother) had sewn them together. "Now look what we have here, ladies and gentlemen: a gift for Our Boys Overseas." Then I had to say the phrase that always stuck in my throat: "It's pretty good, don't you think?" Applause! Applause! I told Mrs. Gore that I didn't think it was the right thing to say, that we seemed to be begging for something. She said, "Nonsense, just say it as it's written, Edward. They'll love it." So I did. And they loved it. They even stood up and applauded. But that was the end of my knitting career.

The odd thing is that I still know how to knit. And now that I'm creeping up toward my seventies, I'm thinking that maybe I'll give it another try.

Please Don't Make Me Knit!

Tara Cibelli

"I think we are going to teach you how to knit," Memere announced.

God! The last thing I wanted to do was knit! I wanted to do everything else but knit. It was the middle of summer! I wanted to swim and play tag with the neighbors. *Anything* but knitting.

"Oh, just try it," Memere insisted. "How do you know you don't like it?"

"Memere," I wailed, "Only OLD people knit. I am only a little girl! I can't knit!"

Memere glared at me with the look that all of us grandchildren feared. The look that said McDonald's was not a possibility for lunch if we did not behave. So my whining did nothing. I sat down with my neon-orange yarn and needles, and I sulked. She was working on an elaborate sweater. She told me to make a scarf for my doll, Kathy. "Making Kathy a scarf is a great project for you!" I sulked some more.

"Keep your fingers loose," Memere instructed, keeping her eyes on my fingers and working her own in a frenzy. "Just concentrate on what you're doing." Knitting had always been something that Memere and Great Memere did together, gossiping in French so that eavesdropping was impossible. But for me, it was a chore. I had to be forced to knit a few clumsy rows of orange for Kathy. Although Memere was a great teacher, wool and needles in 85-degree weather was not my idea of a good time. By the time Memere finished her elaborate sweater, I had completed my scarf for Kathy. It was the most hideous piece of clothing that I could have imagined. Of course Kathy had far too much taste to wear this horrible thing.

That was 12 years ago. I am a senior in college now, and Memere is one of my best friends. Although I have always loved to do a variety of things with Memere, knitting never turned out to be one of them. But her knitting is still part of my life. Mittens, hats and sweaters stemmed from Memere's magic hands, keep me warm year after year.

I haven't tried knitting again—not because I think I wouldn't enjoy it, but because to me, knitting belongs to Memere. I like being measured each year for my sweater and going with her to the yarn shop to pick out the perfect shade of purple. These sweaters need her hands, not mine, for they are a part of her that I can carry with me all the time.

The Knitting Club

Frances Lord Corriveau

I drew closer to examine my mother's latest creations lined up on the kitchen counter. The pastel mounds looked intriguing in their tissue paper nests. I poked one with a grubby finger. "What are these, Mom?"

"Those are for the Church. Please keep fingers off." I withdrew the offending finger.

"What are they *for*, though?"

"Honestly, Liz. I am trying to get dressed."

My mother appeared wearing my favorite blue dress and her Sunday shoes. She was clipping her earrings in place. I smelled the scent of lavender as she moved in close to buss my cheek. "Those are baby booties, honey. I knit them for the Church to give to those babies less fortunate than us." I tried to picture what the babies who were less fortunate than us would look like. We were pretty poor ourselves. Maybe like the children in foreign countries without enough to eat that the pastor talked about last Sunday. "Now you be a good girl and do what your daddy says while I'm gone and tonight we'll play a game." I smiled at my pretty mother with her slim figure and flawless olive skin. She was always inventing games for my friends and me. Some were more fun than others but she never gave up trying.

The booties forgotten, I ran out to play with Larry and Dave. We spent the warm summer afternoon playing cowboys and Indians. I was always the designated Indian. I didn't mind except for the twins' occasional tendency to gang up on me. It was suppertime before I heard my mother calling. It seemed too early to go in but I knew better than to ignore her. I'd gotten in plenty of trouble before doing just that. Besides, my appetite was legendary at that age. "Come on, guys. Maybe she made some cookies."

Dave and Larry looked none too sure of the existence of cookies but they tagged along anyway. They needed their Indian to continue playing. I smelled the hot dogs before I entered our old farmhouse. My dad worked second shift, so we had our big meal at lunch. Mom and I usually had something lighter for supper. "Can Larry and Dave stay, Mommy?"

My mother smiled her splendid smile and nodded. She was a generous woman. The three of us bolted our food and were soon ready to be off again. My mother paused as she cleared the table. "We can play a game later if you'd like."

I nodded slowly. "What kind of game?"

"I thought you children might like to learn to knit."

Larry and I looked at each other. Nothing was farther from our minds on a warm Vermont night. We had exploring to do.

"I'm going to make some popcorn." My mother was an exceptional motivator of hungry children. Grudgingly we agreed, the thought of popcorn irresistible. It wasn't an hour before Mom called again. I ran into the kitchen and there on our old Formica table was a big bowl of popcorn. My smiling mother sat knitting beside it. I stopped short and Larry and Dave crashed into me. "Come in, boys. Go wash your hands and you can have some popcorn. You too, Liz." We piled over to the old marble sink by the stove. I let the cold water out over my hands and dabbed them with soap. Larry and Dave waited to do the same. More or less clean and dry, we returned to the table. "I thought we might start a knitting club this evening. You have been saying that there isn't anything to do this summer. It would be a very nice thing to be able to knit, don't you think?" We nodded, eyeing the popcorn. It was a big draw. I took a place alongside my mother wondering what she could possibly be thinking, trying to teach knitting to rowdy nine-year-olds.

Mom produced a ball of yarn for each of us. Mine was royal blue. That evening, she tried to show us how to cast on, as I remember. I succeeded only in tangling the yarn. My mother was so patient as she unraveled my mess time and again. I hung in there, half-heartedly pushing needles through my yarn until the popcorn was gone. Then Larry started squirming. I figured any good friend would get him out of there, so I thought up something to do. "Larry and I are gonna go outside and play badminton before it gets dark, Mom. Okay?" My long-suffering mother looked at my hopeless tangle of yarn and nodded. Before she could change her mind, Larry and I bolted for the door leaving poor Dave attempting to produce a row of cast-on stitches.

The backyard had only the illumination from the lamp on our dilapidated old porch. It gave a large enough circle of light to play badminton if you didn't hit the birdie too hard. We swatted the thing around until Dave and my mother appeared much later at the door, knitting finished for the evening. Freed from his fate, Dave scooted to join us. My mother gave us a cheery wave and went back into the house.

The next night, my mother didn't even let me out after supper. Instead, she had me call Dave and Larry over to continue the Knitting Club. The same scenario recurred: once the popcorn was gone, Larry and I ran out in the backyard to play badminton in the dark. Poor Dave was too nice a boy to make an escape from my mother. He stuck it out, night after night, learning to knit some slippers. The Knitting Club continued to meet until the summer was almost at an end. One cool August night, Dave finished his slippers. Mom made a big thing of congratulating him. Then she collected all our yarn and put it away. That was the end of the Knitting Club. I never saw that tangle of royal blue yarn again, but I sure did miss the popcorn.

Aunts and Other Friends

Aunt Ruth

Jay Elliott

Forty-five years ago, during my twelfth summer, my Aunt Ruth came to stay with us at our Northern California Sierra foothill town to "lie in" toward the end of her fourth and last pregnancy. She left my three younger cousins with their father in L.A., claiming a need to escape from the July heat of Southern California, but I suspect now she felt more secure being with her big brother, a small-town country doctor, for this was proving to be a difficult pregnancy. Being pathologically shy, I felt some awe before this voluble, attractive woman, who not only seemed to be going overboard by having a fourth child (to my mind three was the absolutely tolerable limit for a woman to achieve), but indulged a ribald sense of humor. "I've found a new use for garbage disposals," she announced when she first appeared, speaking of a new-fangled device that our technologically deficient lives had not yet made the acquaintance of. "It's perfect for grinding up Bill's cigar butts." Then, winking at my father, "And that suggests a more Freudian function if he misbehaves."

I had mixed feelings about her presence, because I was, so to speak, in the same boat. Just after Little League was over, my father had taken me and my two brothers fishing on the American River. With his fly rod, he drifted off downstream, and I dawdled along the huge boulder interfaces, alternating my fishing with prospecting for gold nuggets the 49ers had overlooked. But having just entered one of those adolescent growth spurts, my feet had naturally outpaced the rest of me, and as I tried to move quickly to another vantage point, I tripped on an outcropping. I stuck my right arm down to break the fall, only to jam it into a slot between two immovable pieces of shale. My momentum carried me forward, my arm stayed behind, and the inevitable result was sudden, complete, displaced double fractures of the ulna and radius midway between my wrist and elbow. I remember no pain as I scrambled to the top of a riverside boulder, holding the arm up against the setting sun and hollering at my father's distant figure, "Dad, I think there's something wrong?" The curious S shape of my arm looked unnatural against the sky. Risking his own tumble, he scrambled back along the river, took me to the car, dragged out his medical bag, and pumped some Demerol into me.

The upshot was that, during my aunt's visit, I too was "lying in," burdened with a bulky L-shaped plaster cast that extended from my knuckles to mid-bicep, an unlikely alternative to an eighth-month fetus, but similar in weight; supporting it with a sling proved impossible for more than a few hours.

One beautiful late morning soon after her arrival, I wandered to the patio, having, as usual, nothing to do—any summer plans I had, like swimming, playing baseball, even doing odd jobs for a dollar or two, were clearly impossible. I suddenly came upon my aunt asleep in a lawn chair, her blond hair tousled, her eyes closed, and her hands clasped over her preternaturally large belly. To me she was formidable. She was my father's sister and thus a full participant in that mysterious realm called adulthood, of which I was beginning to get more and more complicated glimpses, but she was also in that unnatural state sometimes cautiously labeled, in the mid-fifties, "with child." I had some knowledge of sexuality from the charts and diagrams cluttering drug company–issued instructional books with neutral titles like *Your Sexuality* and *Sexuality for Teens*, written expressly for adolescents. These slim volumes and pamphlets my father received gratis at the office as advertisements and asked me to "review": "Are these worth handing out to my teenage patients?" he would ask. But as I found myself so closely confronted with an undeniable result of human sexual congress, I realized I knew nothing about the emotions that accompanied any of it. What do I do, I thought, with my own changes? I can name each part, I know how everything works, how everything fits. But how does sex fit with love?

"Good morning," she said with a weary smile, having awakened while I was wool-gathering. "How are you?"

"It itches," I responded curtly, gesturing to my immobilized arm. It was the constant plague of my condition. The summer heat, along with my own darkening and thickening body hair, caused insufferable irritation under the cast, and several times I had contemplated banging the thing on a concrete curb just to see if the jarring would bring some relief. "You'll just have to live with it," my father said when I complained. Then, to Aunt Ruth, as I remembered my manners: "How are you feeling?"

She gazed at me silently for a moment, seeming to sense the underlying urgency behind my commonplace pleasantry, and answered with more detail than I expected. "I've got some pain in my back, and I'm tired all the time, and the baby's really kicking this morning. You know, though, even though it can hurt, it's an exciting feeling. Each child, you know, moves differently in the womb, and sometimes I think I can tell its personality before it's born. Oof!" she cried, "that was a ground-rule double. Really caught hold of that one. Here, come feel it." I timidly approached, reached out my left hand; she grasped my wrist and placed my palm on the shirt covering her swollen belly. The intimate shock of feeling a dull whomp! rising into my sweaty palm through the thin cotton over her sun-warmed skin was electric; the hair on the back of my neck suddenly rose. I had never, in memory, been in such close proximity to the miracle of the unborn, and I caught my breath. I hadn't registered, at six, my youngest brother's birth; I just remembered his sudden, squalling appearance after my mother had disappeared into the hospital for a few days. "Home run, at least," I said with a lopsided grin.

She leaned down and picked up a large bag. "My knitting," she said. "If we two waifs are condemned to suffer out our time, we might as well be constructive about it." Then she looked at my immobile arm with a speculative eye. "You itch? What about this?" She held up one of her knitting needles for me to inspect. "Maybe this will go under the cast?"

Hesitantly, I inserted the needle under the cast above the web of skin between my thumb and index finger. It slid coolly along my arm, flexible enough to move around the slight curves of my wrist and long enough to reach the insanely sensitive spots that were driving me nuts. "Oh," I breathed. "Ahh!"

She was a miracle worker, I decided then and there. For the rest of her visit we two waifs were inseparable. Aunt Ruth taught me bridge and (of course) how to knit, though holding the needle in my constricted right hand was awkward, and the plain, square potholder I produced looked like an antique, it was so full of ready-made moth holes where I'd dropped stitches. More than that, her conversation gave her adolescent nephew sturdy insights into that totally unknown and intimidating realm known as Woman. My mind retains not a jot or tittle of how to knit, but the sight of a prospective mother pulling out her yarn and needles still evokes the deep pleasure of Aunt Ruth and how, click, click, she made that summer fly.

The Yarn That Binds

Kay Dorn

In the summer of 1942, when we were ten, Julie and I declared ourselves best friends. We made an unlikely pair—a southern black, living without electricity at the end of a dirt road, and a northern white, living in Florida temporarily during World War II. Dad, an Army Air Force officer, had transported the family south to be near him.

Mom was expecting, and to help her cope with the heat my parents hired a lady to clean. During the summer, she brought her daughter, Julie, to our house, and we spent our days dressing my dolls and catching lizards. That first summer Mom decided that third grade was a suitable time to teach us to knit. She told us if we finished the place mats we were knitting, we could eat our lunch in the dining room. So we began our garter-stitch journey with size 11 needles. When we completed the rectangles (mine was more a trapezoid), Mom cast off and taught us how to make fringe. "Good thing the hole's in the middle," Julie said, inspecting mine. "It won't show when you put your plate on it."

The next summer, Julie arrived again with her mother, but she had grown quite sassy over the winter. For instance, one morning Mom gave us each a quarter to buy yarn for afghan squares we were to knit for soldiers in military hospitals. While we were at the five and dime I had to go to the rest room and told her it was okay for her to go in the door marked "White Ladies" because she was with me. "What a dumbster," she scowled. "You don't know nothin'." And she ran back to the house alone. And that's the way the summer went—one minute knitting together under the banyan tree, next minute angry at each other. Before summer ended, Mom drove us to the Red Cross to deliver the red, white and blue squares we had knit for the wounded. We held hands all the way home, we were so happy.

But the following summer started out with another argument. "Why don't we make blankets for our dolls like the one Mom knit for the baby?" I suggested. "Dumbster. You don't know nothin'," she said, and spent the rest of the day helping her mother clean our house. Mom knew. Soon after, Julie and I went out to our favorite banyan grove and found two boxes—each contained a baby doll that squeaked when you pressed its tummy. Julie's wore a purple knit hat and sweater; mine wore green. "You made these," Julie said, and hugged my mother. We settled into knitting basket-weave blankets for our babies. Knit five, purl five for five rows, then purl five, knit five. Sometimes I would lose track and knit six, or four. But Julie's rows were always perfect.

During our last summer, Mom wrote simple directions for doll clothes and we learned to cast on and off. Julie even succeeded to increase and decrease. Then, late one August night our family heard the newsboy running down the street shouting, "Extra, Extra, Japan surrenders." Mom and Dad cried with joy. But the next morning Julie and I sat devastated while our mothers talked. We were moving again. "Maybe you could take the train up next summer," I suggested. "Dumbster," she replied, and slammed the screen door as she ran out of the house. I followed her to our knitting tree, and we hugged, swearing we'd be friends forever—a promise I promptly forgot.

In fact, I rarely even thought of her, except once in high school when I knit argyle socks for my boyfriend and a hole in the heel reminded me of the hole in my third-grade place mat. One time I remember Mom saying she had received a letter from Julie, but I was too caught up in wedding plans even to read the note.

Meanwhile, the years passed. My husband and I had four children, all outfitted in my mom's knitting. Then in 1983, my mother died. I was going through her treasures and found a scattering of blue envelopes in the bottom of the inlaid keepsake box Dad had made for her. The elastic that once held them together had disintegrated in the attic heat. They were signed "Julia Ann." I put the notes in order and pieced together Julie's life. She had become a teacher, just as she'd dreamed. "Like your mother," she had said. And guess what her first home economics class made? Place mats for snack time. The memories flared. "Dumbster," I cried, remembering my promises. A thank-you note revealed that Mom had knit baby outfits for her children and her first grandchild. One tattered letter said: "You made me see I could do anything if I tried. I hope I have taught others the joys of knitting as you taught me; and to use their knitting to help others as you showed us so long ago when we knit for the wounded soldiers." Finally, a note from Julie's sister, enclosing her obituary.

Why had I allowed the yarns that bound us to hang loose all those years? But I believe we remained connected spiritually—we must have experienced the same excitement selecting the emerald and gold yarns we fingered; the same satisfaction from teaching others to love knitting; the same joy knitting for our children and grandchildren and the same gratitude that we could make knitted gifts for the needy and sick. I know that the love of wools, cottons and silks my mother shared with Julie and me won't be snipped off like the last thread in a garment. Mom's love of the yarns will continue, through us, to knit people together far into the future.

A Dying Art?

Elaine Lang Greenstein

I've knit since I was a child. So have my sisters. We learned from our mother. We've made countless sweaters, yards of scarves, piles of afghans, and boxfuls of mittens and hats. It never occurred to me there was anything unusual about this. Until the other day when I visited my daughter's first-grade class.

I had arrived early for the field trip I was chaperoning. As usual, I had my knitting with me so I got it out and began working. The next thing I knew, I was surrounded by the curious kids, who crowded in to get a good view. They found the process mysterious and magical. We all know knitting IS mysterious and magical. A single strand of wool is transformed into beautiful and varied patterns just by moving two (or sometimes three) needles in certain ways. A ball of wool becomes a whole new shape and the new creation then has a function familiar to everyone. Knitting truly is amazing and the kids' perceptions helped me rediscover the wonder of it that I've so taken for granted over the past many years.

But what was most striking to me about these 6- and 7-year-old children's reactions was the comment I heard most frequently: "My grandmother knits." Not a single kid told me about a mother (not to mention a father) who knits. I began to wonder. Does this mean most of my generation doesn't know how to knit, or just doesn't knit? And if they don't knit, will their kids learn how? And if the next generation doesn't learn how, will the art of knitting die out?

I hope the phenomenon I observed is particular to upper-middle-class neighborhoods like the one my daughter's school is in. I hate the thought that all over the world there are fewer and fewer people passing down the wondrous art of knitting from one generation to the next.

Right now, I have two sets of size 10 needles and two big balls of yarn at the ready. This weekend I will give my first knitting lesson to my first-grader and her fourth-grade sister.

A Sister's Socks

Kathryn Gunn

Today is ANZAC Day—the 25th of April—a day on which Australians and New Zealanders remember their servicemen, in particular the landing at Gallipoli in World War I. Yesterday I went to visit one of the old people I like to keep an eye on, Arthur McLean. Having just come out of hospital, he's not well enough to join in the armed services march today, but he was watching me knit and told me this story: "You know when one of my mates was dying out there in the trenches, he gave me the socks his sister had made for him. They were great socks, not those flimsy things you buy in the shops. When I came back I went looking for that girl—and I married her. You know, it was all because of a pair of socks. I've never had any other sort of socks." He was married to Elizabeth, his sock knitter, for 51 years.

Aunt Germaine

Jennifer Hope

My last conversation with Aunt Germaine was about knitting. More than eighty years old and slowly dying of cancer, she wanted to know more about my knitting machine, which had rekindled my passion for knitting. "How do you cast on?" she asked in her fragile voice. As best I could, I tried to explain the process. I know she was only hearing a small portion of what I was saying, but it didn't matter. I was amazed that, as small and fragile as she had become, her mind was still functioning and she was still curious.

In 1963, when my parents divorced, the judge awarded custody of my sister and me to our father, leaving us motherless. My grandfather's sisters, Aunt Germaine and Aunt Velma, took us in after school and on weekends while my father was working. One autumn afternoon when I was six, I sat mesmerized by my aunt's knitting needles. She made such beautiful things—sweaters, doll clothes, skirts; she even knitted a winter coat. I was curious about knitting and I asked her to teach me. She gathered together some needles and a skein of yellow yarn and, with the patience of Job, taught me my first knit and purl. We made a pair of mittens that afternoon while my father, an avid photographer at the time, snapped pictures. I've long since lost the mittens but still have the photos. My face is taut with concentration as I sit on Aunt Germaine's lap, her arms encircling me, guiding my efforts.

Another rainy autumn day a few years later, we took the bus uptown to her favorite yarn shop. Along the way we gathered leaves and met a man who grew giant dahlias in his backyard. My memories of Aunt Germaine, like those days, are sweet.

I learned more than a simple craft from her. I learned the value of problem-solving. I learned how to persevere until the job's done (although you wouldn't know it judging my collection of unfinished projects). I learned to be patient with myself. I learned a little math. I learned to be proud of my work. . . . I learned to knit.

Thank you, Aunt Germaine. I love you.

The Challenge of YO

Jackie Young

For many years now, a group of friends has gathered every Thursday evening for crafting and talk. We knit, crochet, spin yarn, laugh over the funny stories and cry when life doles out trouble. One friend in our group is a spinner. No spinning job is too big for Connie. She can spin silk, dog hair, cotton, flax, wool and assorted unknown fibers. She uses a drop spindle, an antique walking wheel or the latest spinning wheel design. Undaunted by any new spinning challenge, Connie constantly amazes us with the yarn she seems to create out of thin air. But when it comes to knitting, her confidence dissolves as quickly as she spins. Even the most basic pattern stumps her. She constantly wails, "What are all those begs and decs? What's a YO?!" We often help her struggle through a pattern, but, always frustrated, Connie goes back to her spinning, adding to the ever-growing mountain of handspun yarn she stores in baskets all over her house.

One year, Connie had to have surgery. We knew she would be facing weeks of bed rest and would not be able to spin. We wondered what we could give her to keep her busy. At last we came up with an idea: a pattern for a vest that she could knit—with no begs, decs or YOs!

Sweater Girls

Linda Quigley

It was inevitable that the day would come when four girls, who had spent childhood summers as inseparable best friends, riding bicycles and horses by day and sleeping in jungle hammocks in the backyard by night, would be steered toward womanhood. Forty years later, I don't know whether that turning point came too soon or too late. Seventh grade was winding down. The days dragged, and we ached for long days and idle hours to explore the woods and creeks and sleep under the stars.

Then, without warning, the promise of the summer of 1961 was hanging by a thread—or, literally, a piece of yarn. What we would do that summer, our parents told us, was learn to knit. Worse, we would learn on Saturday mornings. "Knit? No-o-o-o-o-o-o!" we cried. Yes, they said, we were going to knit and we were going to become proper young ladies. Even at 12, I could've told my parents that one out of two was the best they could hope for. I might manage to knit a sweater, but propriety was not in the cards. The prognosis was similar for Jan, Jennie and Lynn. But through some network that remains a mystery today, our four families agreed we had squandered enough summers building treehouses and shooting cans with BB guns and engaging in other pursuits hardly suitable for their sons and certainly not for their daughters.

The plot came to fruition when we arrived for the first Saturday lessons at The Knit Shop, a tree-shaded storefront just off the main street of our Southern hometown. Gertrude Landers, the pleasant, apple-cheeked owner, welcomed us as if we were prize pupils. "Girls, I am delighted you have come to be taught the art of knitting, one of the skills you must have to express your womanhood." She told us this with what was, as nearly as I could tell, absolute sincerity. She introduced us to Rae Anderson, a British woman with an accent nothing less than exotic, there on the banks of the Tennessee River. Mrs. Anderson would teach us the womanly skill of knitting, and her thoughts about the subject echoed those of Mrs. Landers. "Knitting is an art that you must have if you are ever to become proper," she said, as if she couldn't look at us and tell that the possibility of that happening was already in serious jeopardy. I had put my favorite army surplus camouflage shirt on over my blue oxford-cloth shirt and denim shorts. Lynne was wearing her brother's football jersey. Jan and Jennie wore blue jeans with the legs rolled up to reveal high-top Converse basketball sneakers. Anyone could see that the gap between what we were and what the ladies at The Knit Shop were charged with helping us become could not be bridged with a skein of wool and a pair of #10 needles.

But that's what each of us was handed as we began to learn to cast on, a term that, up to that point, we had used only in relation to fishing lines. Mrs. Anderson would lean forward and examine our work, admonishing us to pull the yarn evenly so each stitch matched the previous one. We were experts at lashing jungle hammocks to tree trunks, so how hard could this be, huh?

"Okay, now, let's unravel all of this and do it again," Mrs. Anderson told us.

"How come?" I mumbled.

"Speak up," she said.

"How come we gotta do it again?"

She stared at me, her hands folded in her lap, her legs crossed at the ankles. "We will do it again," she said in her clipped British accent, "because that is the way we learn. We do it over and over until it is perfect." Jan, Jennie, Lynne and I looked at each other, then slipped the carefully cast-on stitches off the needle, pulled the yarn as gently as we could to straighten it and picked it up again.

It was a long morning, the first in a series of long mornings. This would gravely limit our weekend activities, the success of which we measured by the number of miles covered on our bicycles and the number of fish and turtles we caught in Blue Creek. But we were told that we would knit, and so we did. I'm sure that there must have been a scarf first, but if there was, it has been lost to both memory and memorabilia. The first sweater, however, still exists, four decades later.

Once we realized we were not going to get out of this scheme to refine us, we set a goal: We would each complete a hand-knit sweater to wear to the much-anticipated Thanksgiving football game between our school and our hated across-the-river rivals. Rough-and-tumble as we were, this was years before Title IX, so the closest we could come to the football field was as spectators. And, truth be told, our hormones were kicking in, and we were eyeing the boys on the field with an interest that was new to us, although we couldn't quite acknowledge that yet without serious embarrassment. Some of what was going on was discussed in a booklet that we had been given in Girl Scouts called *Growing Up and Liking It*, which included the topics of menstruation and breasts. Even with our ambivalence, we concluded that there was no better way to show off our developing bodies and our personal style than in handmade sweaters.

Unfortunately, the pattern we selected—yes, each of us decided on exactly the same sweater—was something Lana Turner would not have been caught dead in. The back and the front had four large squares each, two alternating colors knitted checkerboard fashion. The front was divided with a contrasting vertical cable; each sleeve was half one color and half the other. The fringe around the hem and the sleeves matched the cable color—in my case, a near-neon coral. My squares were a more muted milk chocolate offset by beige heather. Jennie had fuchsia cable and fringe, with teal blue squares and the same beige that I used. The other two combinations, while not enshrined in my memory, were no doubt just as striking.

As the sweaters took shape, our commitment grew beyond the two-hour lessons. Soon, a couple of times during the week, I'd voluntarily drag my knitting bag out and add an inch to one of those brown squares. By the next Saturday morning, I would've made enough progress that Mrs. Anderson, the Queen of Purls, was nearly convinced I could become a lady. I did a pretty good job with the knit-purl part, but the cable hook threw me. I could tie a horse to a post or a boat to a dock, but to twist yarn around that little curve of metal, and to lace it back properly without ending up with a big hole was tough. Over and over I did it, until I got it right. It was the womanly way, of course. Knit. Purl. Increase. Decrease. Repeat. Words in our vocabulary took on new meanings as our sweaters grew.

Finally, there came a Saturday when we went back to my house and knitted all afternoon. Our parents thought that their mission to mold us into some semblance of proper womanhood had been accomplished, and we were beginning to look at each other with some suspicion that they might be right. When our sweaters were finally finished and properly blocked (another new word, until then associated with our backyard football games), we each chose fabric for our mothers to make our skirts. They were all alike, lightweight wool with stitched-down pleats, each matching the darkest color in the sweater it would be worn with. We counted the days until Thanksgiving.

That November, we polished our penny loafers, washed our hair and dressed, and Lynne and her dad picked us up one by one for the ride to the stadium. Lynne's dad warned us of the possibility of rain.

"If it starts to rain, I'll pick you up," he said. "Where the hell are your raincoats? Didn't anybody bring a raincoat?" he asked as we tumbled out of the car. Why, for goodness' sake, would we put on raincoats to cover up our sweaters, our beautiful foursquare sweaters? Today I close my eyes and try to think of what we must have looked like walking side by side into the stadium, four abreast. Those meeting us saw sixteen multicolored wool squares and those behind us sixteen more. No one looked us in the eye. Before the first quarter ended, the skies opened up. We looked at each other solemnly as the smell of wet wool reached our nostrils. In pouring rain, we walked out of the stadium, sixteen multicolored squares, darker and snugger now than when we'd come in.

Lynne's dad was at the curb, and we piled into the car silently. Graciously, he did not comment on the wet dog smell that we brought with us. He took us back to Lynne's house. We all changed into Lynne's clothes (okay, some of us changed into her brother's clothes) and decided we'd go to the movie. There were no westerns showing, so we chose Elvis Presley's *Blue Hawaii*, which, under different circumstances, might have also signaled a step forward in the feminine arena. The skirt and sweater combination outfitted us for success in the coming teenage years. Something had gone terribly wrong. We didn't know yet what it was, but we were convinced it had begun with knitting.

The Guys in Our Lives

This Afghan

Miriam Lang

The most significant thing about this afghan has always been that I made it for us. We had just fallen in love when I saw the pattern book of fisherman's afghans and I knew right away that I wanted to make one to keep folded at the foot of our bed. I could envision just how it would wait there, softly, ready to embrace us should we need an extra layer as we lay embracing each other. Of course, my family scoffed. They didn't think much of my relationship with David and they predicted that I'd never finish the afghan.

But they were wrong about the afghan. I chose a pattern made of 6-inch squares. I could easily carry a piece with me to classes. I knit my way through school from winter into spring, only occasionally dropping a cable needle that rang on the linoleum, calling the professor's attention to my peripheral activity. School was undemanding, in any case. I much preferred thinking about David to thinking about classification schemes or specialized indices. I imagined our future together with every stitch, wound my dreams into every cable, embellished them in each bobble.

By June the afghan was completed. I sewed the squares together, made the fringe and showed it to David. "Too hot," he pronounced it. I swallowed my disappointment and folded it gently, among mothballs, to wait for cooler weather.

The weather cooled, of course, but so did David's ardor. My family was right about that, at least.

Now I huddle in my bed, solitary, wrapped in our afghan. I must acknowledge that it was never our afghan, only mine. Whatever expectations I knit into it were one-sided. David didn't choose the pattern or agree that I should knit it. I made the entire thing myself. Small wonder that he was unwilling to use it.

It is, nonetheless, a comfort. And, I think, beautiful. It is nothing to be ashamed of, though I use it alone.

Warm Neck, Warm Heart

Christine G. Hagan

It was my second year in college, and Christmas was coming, facing me with a serious question: What was I going to give the young man who had captured my heart? I didn't have much money, but I wanted to give him something that showed I cared. I had often knit when I was younger, but college had taken so much of my time that I had found little time to pick up my needles. But then an idea came to me. This was the end of the 1960s and long top coats on young men were in fashion. I decided I would knit him a long scarf to go with his top coat.

Since he was tall, I bought quite a bit of yarn. Then I decided to try those new one-piece needles that everyone was raving about. Reassured by the other knitters in the dorm that I had enough yarn, I set about making time to knit. Well, I knitted while I studied; I knitted while I listened to lectures; I knitted long into the night, after everyone had gone to bed. Those new one-piece needles were something! My fingers really flew—until the day, a week before Christmas, when I actually took a good look at this scarf. I had very little yarn left, but the scarf didn't seem anywhere near long enough. My knitting friends looked in my knitting bag and pulled out the work that I'd been laboring over for weeks. When they held it up, I almost died. There, in front of me, was the widest scarf I had ever seen. It was wide enough to be a skirt for me. I hadn't really paid a great deal of attention to the number of stitches I was casting on; instead, I was concentrating on not twisting the yarn as I joined the cast-ons on my needles. Once I had the stitches on, and they weren't twisted, I was so relieved that I just knit away.

It was a disaster, or so I thought. The other girls and I agreed we would have to rip the whole scarf out and I would have to start all over again. I couldn't bear to rip it out, so I went for a walk around the dorm while they pulled the scarf apart and rewound the yarn. When I came back, they sat with me while I cast on a more reasonable number of stitches. Then I started over, with *very* little time left before Christmas.

That night, I saw the musical *West Side Story* for a theater class I was taking. Needles(s) to say, the scarf went with me. I sat there and knit flat-out, all the way through the play. Thank goodness I had decided to make the scarf plain! The musical was a long one, and I got quite a bit done. Every day after that, my hands just flew with those needles. Finally, I decided, with one day to go, that the scarf for my young man was just the right length. I was rushed for time, but I got the fringe on, cut it, and wrapped the package, just as he arrived at my house on Christmas Eve.

Of course, he loved it. He was too nice to say otherwise. Was it a disaster, having to take the scarf apart and start over? I don't think so. There wasn't anything I wouldn't have done for this young man. I guess he felt the same way, since we married shortly after graduation and have just celebrated 28 wonderful "tightly knit" years together. He still has that scarf, and he still has me.

All those years ago I warmed his neck and—little did I know at the time—his heart as well.

Knitting for Love

Mary Keenan

It all began innocently enough. Throw a hundred girls into a university residence, and you're bound to find a few who know how to knit. Those of us from small towns had sustained ourselves for years with faded acrylics and chunky wools, so you could hardly expect us to resist the seductively compact balls of crisp amber or magenta fluff offered in the now accessible local specialty stores. Nor could you expect other girls, watching these colorful strings climb a pair of pointed sticks, to view the finished product and not want a trim little vest or frothy cardigan of their own. Before long, our residence was a hotbed of competitive knitting.

I was one of the early contenders. *Vogue Knitting*, which I had never seen before, was suddenly available everywhere, and I had discovered an outlet store where beautiful wool could be had at bargain prices. I was also fairly experienced, having produced several sweaters for myself and another enormously long one, with a color block and a cable, for a 6'2" boyfriend. Even so, my credits paled in comparison to those of another girl in my year who was skilled and, above all, fearless. During our first month at college, this girl brought home an enormous quantity of black and white yarn. It seemed far too much for one sweater. Clutching our copies of *Vogue Knitting*, we asked her what she was planning to make. The answer bowled us over. She was embarking on the one sweater we all loved but did not dare consider: a cropped boxy pullover with a complex houndstooth check. She finished it without difficulty and in no time she was wearing this striking garment everywhere, with layers piled up underneath as the weather grew cold. It was like a red flag to the rest of us. If she could make that sweater, then the sky was the limit.

My own specialty became cables. I found that, since everyone else had taken the color route, the sight of a double-ended needle falling forward and back to create an intricate Aran pattern earned me a certain novelty value amongst the growing number of knitters. By January, we were freely skipping our evening classes in favor of coaxing a piece as far as the cast-off stitches for its armhole. We checked on each other's progress the way new mothers do with babies, admiring appearances and politely inquiring about length and age.

As our personal sweater collections outgrew our closets, the competition spilled over into our love lives. We assessed the men on campus not by their looks or intellectual prowess, but by the length of their arms. Foolishly, I had taken on another 6'2" boyfriend and cursed myself for it as I feverishly produced a pair of his-and-hers Aran sweaters. Still, I was one of the lucky ones. I was able to participate in collective head-shaking over other girls who, battling the twin perils of infatuation with a guy and obsession with a new pattern, started measuring him too soon. A case in point was the girl who learned to knit just to make mittens for her new boyfriend. It was a definite risk—mittens might not mean much in themselves, but the fact that she had never knit before meant a lot. The mittens were still unfinished when the man in question broke off their relationship and, ironically, fell in love with the girl who had made the houndstooth sweater.

Old habits die hard, and even after I left dorm residence for an apartment of my own I went on knitting. I'd met someone new, yet another 6'2" man who was, to make matters worse, significantly bulkier through the body than my two previous boyfriends. This time I resisted knitting for him, producing instead a regular supply of niece-size Icelandic sweaters. But when we were parted for six months I found myself so bereft that I devoted all my free time to making him the best sweater I could imagine. In the end, it was a triumph of devotion: an off-white wool tent with a chevron pattern of minute intricacy. After we broke up, he returned the sweater and I wore it myself for a short time, swimming in it and vowing to make it again, but smaller, for myself. Then I gave it back and this time he didn't argue.

By the time I met my husband, who is 5'10", I had inherited a sewing machine and was knitting less than before. One day, however, he asked me to make something especially for him. Knowing he does not readily wear sweaters of any kind, I gave him my collection of knitting magazines and vintage patterns and told him to choose one. He looked everything over, rejecting all the things I would have loved to knit, then showed me a child's cardigan illustrated by a round mother duck being trailed by her offspring. I couldn't believe it. For once I'd fallen in love with a sensibly sized man, and he not only wanted me to adapt this child's cardigan into an adult's pullover, he wanted the one type of project I had far from perfected.

Of course, I made him the sweater, struggling to keep my stitches flat as I brought in patches of bright yellow yarn. I even extended the parade of baby ducks across the back, punctuating it with one tardy duckling in an orange toque that matched the one my husband wears to play hockey. It looked ridiculous, and it took a long time to finish. But one beautiful fall day, he took me to a harvest festival and wore the sweater, proudly telling everyone who commented—and somehow, almost everyone we met commented—that I had made it for him. I may have shown my love for him by knitting a sweater covered with ducks, but on that day, my husband more than showed his for me by wearing it.

Revenge: Warm and Custom-Fitted

Caroline Laudig

About twenty-four years ago, I graduated from college and married Michael, my college sweetheart. Since he was in the Navy and living at the naval air station in Millington, just north of Memphis, Tennessee, I quit my job and moved from Indianapolis to live with him in base housing. At the time, I was weaving a lot, but I still kept my hand in at knitting. It's usually too hot in Memphis, even in December, to think about knitting a huge wooly sweater. I stuck mostly to my embroidery and sewing.

The winter we were there, however, the Mississippi froze in spots as far south as Memphis. So, I looked into my sweater pattern library and considered knitting Michael a sweater for Christmas. I decided to knit him an Icelandic yoke sweater in bulky, lightly spun Lopi yarns. Since we were newlyweds, living in base housing, and he was a low-ranking non-commissioned officer in the Navy, we were on an extremely tight budget. I managed to save enough money to buy the yarn out of our already minuscule grocery budget by using coupons for everything. (This was in the days when the grocery store actually gave you cash back for the coupons!)

It took me about a week of concentrated knitting to finish Michael's sweater, which had all the custom touches you would expect. Since he was more than six feet tall, it was more like knitting acreage than knitting a "size." The arms fit him exactly. I added short rows just above the ribbed waistband so that it wouldn't ride up on him and expose his back. There were additional short rows at the back of the neck to shield that delicate area from a cold draft. He loved that sweater and wore it at every possible opportunity. I showed him how to take care of it, wash it, de-pill it, store it between seasons. I even demonstrated how to fold it. Whenever he was away on assignment, I was assured that he could take care of the sweater properly, and he always did.

Then he asked for another. I was flattered and knitted a second one. Then a third, fourth and fifth one. Then his friends wanted sweaters, so for a short time I was selling them as fast as I could knit them. Then he wanted a cabled sweater, and showed me pictures of sweaters he had seen in catalogs. So I knitted him an Aran-style sweater, and another, and another. Don't get me wrong—I loved knitting. In fact, I eventually abandoned the weaving entirely to devote myself to knitting. And Michael waited on me, hand and foot, while I immersed myself in the pleasures of knitting a sweater for him. Sometimes I'd even drag out the knitting process so that he would cook and do laundry for an additional week.

Then, after eight years of marriage, we got divorced.

The divorce itself was fairly amicable. We divided our household in a single tight-lipped session of "that's mine, this is yours." He got everything that was his before the wedding; I got all my antique furniture back. We seemed to manage pretty well UNTIL we got to the sweaters. Bear in mind that I am short and Rubenesque. Michael was tall and stocky. Not only did I not really WANT the sweaters, they really would have been no use to me at all. I couldn't have worn them, and they were felted together enough from regular wear that I didn't want to unravel them for the yarn. The sweaters were being stored at my mother's house, and something compelled me to get them and put them where Michael couldn't find them. Then I told him that because I had knitted them, the sweaters reverted to me. This was, of course, a ploy to get him to work up some emotion over them. I made sure that we had a terrific row over them, hoping that he would want them so much that he would never get rid of them. It worked. We fought back and forth for about a week, then I finally made a big show of relenting. I wrapped the sweaters carefully, with lots of cedar chips, and I threw in the pair of hunting socks I had also knitted for him. I delivered them to his mother's house, making sure that she noted how carefully they were wrapped and handled. I delivered them without acrimony or recriminations, but I made sure that he understood how much of a loss I felt this was, giving up my handwork.

Now, sixteen years later, I know he thinks about me when he puts on one of those sweaters before he goes out in the cold.

Love and Lace

Susan Lydon

For the past couple of years, I've been knitting lace shawls. I recently finished up my third version of the Kerry Blue Shawl from Martha Waterman's book *Traditional Knitted Lace Shawls*. I like this design because it frequently changes pattern, staving off boredom. Each time I've knit this shawl, as well as other smaller lace pieces, I've experimented with degrees of transparency, using larger needles and finer yarn. My aim was to achieve a sheer, diaphanous, almost invisible quality. There is something about the illusion of a weightless little nothing that nonetheless keeps you warm; it appeals to the magician in me. If knitting is a feat of homemade magic, a conjuring trick (and I believe it is), then lace knitting is advanced magic.

Lace forms as the knitter captures emptiness, making holes between the solid stitches in a patterned repetition. How opaque or transparent the resulting fabric becomes is determined by the size and frequency of the holes. The fabric can range from the nearly solid pointelle knit, to the half-solid and half-open eyelet, to the open weave of hairpin lace, in which the solid element comes close to disappearing.

For me, the making of lace is irresistible; its rhythms are compelling, its results spectacular. Thoughts and images flow freely across my mind as I perform the mathematical arabesque of adding and subtracting stitches in a predetermined pattern, counting repetitions and rows as the shawl takes form and grows. I savor the words that occur to me as I knit: cobweb, gossamer, gauze; translucent, delicate, sheer. Meg Swansen says of this refined passion, "As our appetite to acquire new techniques and knowledge becomes more ravenous, it is nearly inevitable that the True Knitter will eventually turn to Knitted Lace."

I began my first shawl with a fine merino in an off shade of blue. I was in the heady early stages of a new relationship and excited about learning a new knitting technique. Of course love is at least as elusive and even more a mystery and magic trick than knitting lace. As Tom Robbins wrote in *Still Life with Woodpecker*, "Who knows how to make love stay?" I tried to teach myself both love and lace with that fine blue shawl, as it went from the inner circle of its beginning to the wavy border of its outer edges, improvising the technical parts I failed to master—with mixed results. That first shawl was thicker than the ones that came after, and the border was sewn onto the edge, but it was beautiful and I felt an enormous satisfaction in having completed it. The man in my life liked it too.

I found I loved the lace: its complex interplay of light and dark, fullness and emptiness, solidity and flimsiness, the way it held both air and space. I enjoyed the way you could see through the whole, like light filtered through a lace curtain. Emptiness expands the mind, the moment, the consciousness of the meditator to allow contemplation of the infinite, the unseen, the larger cosmic view of life. Emptiness also expanded the shawl. It was composed of four triangles, gradually increasing with yarnovers on either side of four central ribs. The yarnover increases enlarged the knitted lace from twelve stitches at its inception to nearly a thousand stitches at its outward edge. At the same time, love expanded my heart and stretched my capacity to experience both pleasure and pain, leaving devastating stretches of emptiness when it left and solid bits of happiness when it returned.

There is a kind of netting milliners use for veils called illusion netting; it is transparent enough to show the face, yet also covers and acts as a scrim, the merest barrier between observer and the observed. Lace creates that same illusion. It also serves similar purposes at the ritual moments of our lives. Consider the veil, which is worn primarily for weddings and funerals. The bridal veil both conceals and reveals the bride, with a tantalizing promise of seduction and virginity. The mourning veil, by contrast, protects the mourner, providing a hiding place for the ravages of grief. Who can forget the image of Jacqueline Kennedy, her eyes red and features swollen, behind her sheer black veil at the funeral of her murdered husband?

Lace is particularly associated with the wedding ceremony. Joni Mitchell's "Song for Sharon," from her album *Hejira*, explores love's illusions. In it she refers to "the long white dress of love" and "the ceremony of the bells and lace." The second shawl I knitted was white. I was at the stage of my relationship where the question of marriage had arisen, and although the shawl was for the wife of my massage therapist, Michael, rather than for myself, I held the question of marriage in my mind as I knitted. I used a finer yarn and larger needles, and the bigger the shawl got, the fluffier and lighter it seemed to become, absorbing air and loft and space. It had an almost magical presence, frothy and confectionery like a wedding cake. When I presented it to Michael, he remarked on how beautiful it was. "It was like knitting a cloud," I said.

The third shawl I knitted was black; I was in mourning. My lover had left me for another woman and I had a permanent hole in the center of my being. I held tight to a passage from a song by Paul Simon, "Graceland," that expressed exactly how I felt: "Everybody sees you're blown apart/ Everybody sees the wind blow." That kind of emptiness was hard to bear. Through heartbreak, I had become a piece of lace myself.

The black shawl was more technically accomplished than the other two. A woman at a knitting retreat I led in Big Sur had showed me how to knit the border directly onto the shawl, so the finished piece had a better drape and finish than the other two. And of course it completed a cycle in my personal life.

Of the three, I loved the fluffy white cloud shawl the best. A year after I had finished it, I had an appointment with Michael. He told me his wife had devised a winter outfit to wear at home that included the shawl. By this time my relationship with the same man had inexplicably revived. Perhaps my next shawl could suggest the image of a phoenix rising.

"I was thinking about marriage when I made that shawl," I told Michael. "The idea of marriage, even though it didn't work out."

"It represents the image well," said Michael. "And after all, you never know."

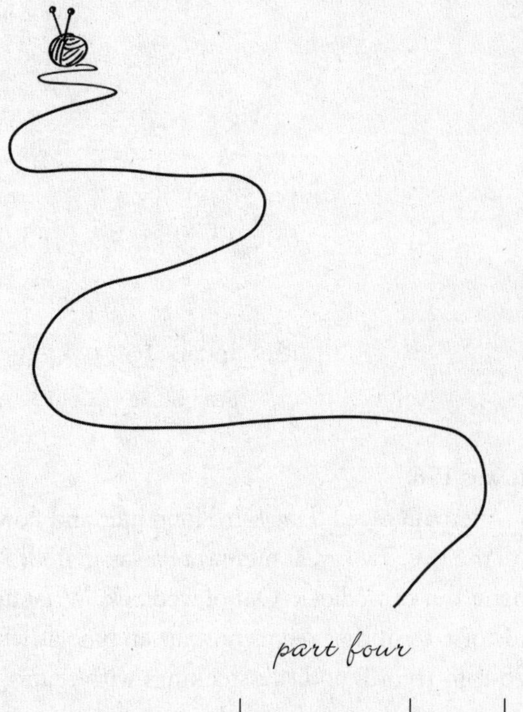

part four

lives and souls

The Baby Blanket

Jean Stone

It was 1968.

Vietnam raged. *Laugh-In,* long hair and flower power were on the rise. Two great men were assassinated. And I was pregnant, out of wedlock. Out of wedlock. What an ancient, prehistoric term that seems now, as archaic as white gloves and 78-rpm records and silk stockings with seams, for those who can remember, for those who were raised reciting the Pledge of Allegiance and who did not quite sync with hippies and free love.

But in 1968, "out of wedlock" was, for good girls (of which I was one) from good families (of which I was a member), the kiss of social death. And though knitting did not change my situation, it provided a focus for my fears and tears, a way to create something good out of the sorrow. It was thirty years before I knew the outcome.

"Don't You Want Somebody to Love," the Jefferson Airplane wailed in the tiny, chintz-papered bedroom of the country house where I'd been sent. I lay on the small twin bed and stared up at the slanted dormer ceiling, trying to decide if I preferred this music to Johnny Mathis or a rah-rah Beach Boys tune. The clash of cultures within my generation often was confusing to the twenty-year-old me. But yes, I wanted somebody to love. I had a baby growing somewhere, somehow, inside me and I wanted very much to love him. I wanted to have the chance. But I did not want to marry the baby's father; he was a boy in college who I barely knew. In 1968, however, a girl "had to" be married to raise a baby. (It is a concept that today feels as foreign to me as it does to the new generation. Did we really live that way? Was society so cruel? The answer, simply put, is Yes.) I was not strong enough to go against my world, a world in which good girls from good families gave up their babies for adoption and went back to their good lives.

"You can give your baby one of two things," the matter-of-fact state social worker had said earlier that day. I had been directed to an uncomfortable wooden chair set in the middle of a drab cinderblock office. Apparently I could not give up my baby without the added humiliation of judgmental social workers ensconced in ugly, unfriendly buildings. "Many girls give their baby a layette." I was ashamed to admit I did not know what a layette was. Then again, I was ashamed of most things those days. And her reference to "many girls" only conjured images of two girls from high school—two girls with "reputations" who had mysteriously left school, one to study "somewhere in Europe," the other to "care for a sick aunt." No, I was not one of "many girls," was I? I had not been hidden at a dreaded home for unwed mothers; I was living with trusted, caring friends of my parents, albeit in another state, far from the eyes of family and neighbors and anyone who might find out. Or who might simply whisper. "What else?" I asked. I could not bring myself to ask what was the other thing that I could give my baby, because I could not say the words "my baby" without breaking down, and good girls did not cry, at least, not in front of strangers. "You can make something. Booties or a sweater. Or a blanket, if you'd like. Do you know how to knit?"

Back in my room, the music stopped. I sat up on the bed and looked down at a paper bag that rested on the floor. The bag read "Ye Olde Yarn Shoppe." I had stopped there after leaving the social worker's gloomy office. Slowly, I reached down and opened the bag. I'm sure I held my breath a moment. Then I pulled out one skein after another. The yarn was thick and white. It was the softest yarn I'd ever touched, yarn like velvet and silk and sweet angora all rolled into one. I held it to my cheek. It was the perfect yarn to weave a blanket to protect my baby from cold and pain and life.

The weeks passed. Often, as I sat in the small room working on the blanket, I paused and looked out the window and up into the sky. I watched as summer turned to autumn and then to winter. And all the while I wondered what my baby would look like and if he'd be smart and if he would be healthy. I hoped he would be a boy, for all the outdated, sexist reasons—all the beliefs that said a boy would be stronger than a girl, stronger in body, mind and spirit. That he would be better equipped to be a special child, an adopted child. I pictured him looking like my father, because I loved my father deeply, and I was so sad this had upset him. I envisioned my happy, healthy baby boy, and I kept on knitting, as if each knit and purl would solidify his life and show him that I loved him, that he would never need to feel alone. It seemed a small, inconsequential gift, but it was all I had to give.

Just before Christmas the blanket was complete. I brought it with me to the hospital. My son was born the day after Christmas 1968. I was not allowed to see him. It would not be fair, the social workers said. It's better this way. I don't know if it was or not. But on the day I left the hospital, an unknowing nurse approached. She wore a bright smile as I was wheeled from my room. "Where's your baby?" she asked. "Are you going to get him now?" I did not smile in return. Instead, I handed her the blanket, the softest, sweetest bundle that I had ever touched.

In 1998, my son turned thirty years old. The Jefferson Airplane was long defunct, and new music sung by groups with names I can't remember filled the airwaves of the young. As I took down the Christmas decorations, I decided to search for my son. And then I wrote a letter.

The day that he agreed to meet me was second in joy only to the day I saw him. It was the day before Valentine's Day 1999. He is a tall man, handsome and very, very smart. He looks like my father, especially his blue, blue eyes. I wonder if I willed that. He has had a good life, raised by the loving parents that I had so hoped for him. I cannot write these words without tears of gratitude and mother's love.

It was six months after our meeting before I found the courage to ask about the blanket. I guess I feared the answer.

"No," he replied. He knew nothing of the blanket. Nothing was given to his parents. He'd never had a gift from me.

So I'm starting over. It's been a while since I've knitted, so the going is rather slow. My eyes don't work as well as they used to. And he's six-foot-four-inches, so it will take me longer to make something that suits him now. But it will be done, and it will be his. And I hope that it will be the softest, sweetest blanket that he has ever touched.

What I Knitted

Natalie Harwood

My mother has a theory that a person's knitting reveals personality. A person who knits on number 1 needles and does intricate eye-squinting precise work is probably a stingy, mean-spirited skinflint. A person who knits large and loose, she believes, is apt to be a generous, big-hearted soul. I doubt if any survey would validate her theory, but my knitting does reflect some part of myself. I am not a person of extremes, so I have never knit on number 0 or 15 needles and never will. I do not have the perseverance to knit a whole layette, but I'm really generous with the booties and caps. I'll never have the skill for complicated stitches, but I have imaginative ideas, usually brought to fruition in a mundane and unskilled sort of way. Being a New Englander, I don't waste time. My knitting project is always in the bag by my chair, and if I do sit down, my hands will not be idle. So I have knitted for over fifty years, and what I have knitted simply weaves the tale of my life.

I learned to knit from my mother who, bless her heart, would be the first to admit that she's not a perfectionist. (My Aunt Dot did exquisite needlework, had money, and was envied by all—she was a perfectionist!) So I never learned the fine points of knitting and remained, for my lifetime, at the very basic level. I first started in the third grade with a simple pattern: knit four stitches, turn, knit four again, on and on until I had a scarf for my doll, Polly. Back in 1945, girls were not as advanced as third-graders are now. We weren't into rock groups and fancy clothes. We played house with dolls and we were always the mommy taking care of everyone in the family.

I grew up with the Second World War blazing away in Europe. My father was in the audiovisual business, and in the summer was a projectionist for an open-air movie theater on Cape Cod. In those days, 16-millimeter movies came on reels. My father would sit in the booth, thread the projectors, and change reels when the little red star showed up in the right-hand corner of the picture. One Christmas I knitted my father a pair of socks with little projectors on each side. Quite a hit at the Bell and Howell convention, I must say. Of course, Dad never said if they were comfortable. They were just so original! Forget the lumps and bumps and double-knotted ends.

College in the fifties saw us all wearing camel hair coats and scarves knitted in our boyfriends' school colors. Princeton's orange and black was popular, but my buff and blue from Hamilton had some status as well. I went to an all-women's school and it was "in" to knit socks for our boyfriends. Our professors were fairly tolerant; but I do remember one instructor losing his cool when, for the umpteenth time, someone dropped a needle during his lecture. He could expound theorems and fill a blackboard with formulas, but the complexity of the four-needle eight-bobbin sock was beyond him.

After college came marriage and the inevitable baby carriage and baby carriage and baby carriage. I had five children in ten years and my mother began to dread it when I would haul out the baby yarn and begin to knit yet another pair of booties. It got so that I could knit a pair of booties in two days in between all that diaper changing, formula boiling, and nose wiping. Then came the mittens—mittens with stripes, mittens with initials (they got lost anyhow), mittens that looked like bunnies, mittens with cables, mittens with angora trim. And after the first snowfall, the back porch would be covered with wet, soggy mittens. There's nothing like the smell of hand-knit, snow-soaked, wet wool mittens steaming away on the radiator. Finally down-filled waterproof nylon mittens arrived and the days of the wet woolies were gone.

For fifteen years I stayed home and raised five kids. Staying at home with children under the age of four can be a mind-numbing experience and left a lot of time for knitting. I tried my hand at just about everything but the knitted kitchen sink. I knitted place mats, doilies, afghans, baby blankets, gloves, hats, and toys. If only I could have knitted money. We were so poor in those days that I made my own Christmas wrapping, tried to slip instant milk onto the table, and cut the boys' hair myself. I was as utilitarian in these efforts as I am with my knitting.

At last the kids were all in school, I went back to work, and the knitting frenzy cooled. The always-in-progress afghan gathered dust in my knitting basket. It wasn't until the first wedding loomed that I began to knit again in earnest: a lovely white Aran-style coverlet, the first of the wedding presents. Then the weddings came too fast, along with the first grand-babies, and I was back to booties and christening blankets.

One of my daughters is a knitter—actually a much better knitter than I am. She reminds me of Aunt Dot; she is careful and precise and takes out her mistakes, no matter how far back she has to go. Her sweaters are masterpieces of precision. I envy the quality of her work. My works are masterpieces of imagination and haste, monuments to my impatience. But I continue to knit. The ever-present afghan gets picked up every month or so, and the doll clothes appear for the grand-daughters, the baby booties for new mothers, blankets and shawls for the elderly.

My neighbor across the street was in her nineties when I visited her for the last time. She was finishing up an afghan square and she said to me rather sadly, "This is my last afghan." She died the following year. I am resolved never to say, "This is my last afghan." When the Lord comes to take me away, I'll just look up and say, "But I'm not finished with my afghan! Just two more squares!"

Canada, East to West

Sallie McFague

I knitted my first sweater when I was eight years old. Or, more accurately, the knitting fairies and I made it. I worked on the sweater during the day, completing a tangled, holey inch or so, and during the night while I slept the knitting fairies not only corrected my mistakes but added another inch or so of flawless knitting. Thus, knitting had an early magic for me: stick with knitting and somehow the holes and tangles will be made right.

It's important that my knitting lesson took place in Canada, for many skeins of knitting yarn were to lead me, like Hansel and Gretel's white pebbles, back to that country after almost fifty years. My knitting lesson began in New Brunswick, on the Bay of Fundy, where my family owned a cottage. After a long detour in Nashville, Tennessee, I knitted my way back to Vancouver, British Columbia, where my knitting is at long last sorting through some of the holes and tangles.

In New Brunswick, I knitted off and on during my teen years and early adulthood, using only the splendid homespun yarns from the Cottage Craft Shop in St. Andrews, the nearby village. This yarn had (and still has) luscious colors with splendid names: Robin's Egg Blue, Goldenrod Yellow, Briar Rose, Live Lobster, Quoddy Blue, and Fundy Fog. The yarn comes in skeins, not balls; it has to be wound into a ball, using a chair back, a friend's hands, or a special yarn roller that my father invented and built. The yarn still contains small bits of tick from the sheep and it is practically indestructible. Until a few years ago I had a sweater I made in high school (I graduated in 1951). And my teddy bear still wears a red homespun sweater I made for him while listening to the Saturday afternoon opera in college.

After I stopped smoking and my sweater production picked up speed (knitting is an excellent substitute for this addiction), family members and friends tried to tell me tactfully that they had enough sweaters. This is understandable, since Nashville weather only permits wearing sweaters a few months of the year. I yearned to knit a sweater in heavy two-ply homespun yarn, but only one of my students, who was planning to spend a year in Scotland, wanted one. At any rate, my production level was causing a glut. What was I to do with all these sweaters?

Then I recalled that the Cottage Craft Shop employed knitters to make sweaters on consignment. The shop provided the yarn and paid the knitter a small sum. Eureka! An outlet for my hobby with no expense and even a small profit! Alas, when I offered my services to the shop I was told that the import and export duties to send yarn and finished sweaters across the border would destroy the profits. However, at about this time I met my partner who—miraculously—lived in Vancouver. Thus, during the long-distance part of our relationship, she became my secret messenger, smuggling yarn in her suitcase from Canada to Nashville and spiriting finished sweaters back over the border. The illegal "drop" became her apartment, with her sneaking duty-free goods over the border and me knitting for a Canadian firm without a working permit. It was the closest I have ever come to criminal behavior and it made me nervous every time I met the eyes of a customs officer. Surely they could tell I was an illegal alien without working papers?

Now I am with my partner as a permanent resident of Canada and happily knitting away with neither guilt nor fear. I'm legal again. The magic I felt almost fifty years ago about Canada and knitting has come full circle. A thread of yarn followed me all these years, finally pulling me back to the land of "peace, order, and good government" (the Canadian equivalent of "life, liberty, and the pursuit of happiness").

Knitting is an orderly, peaceful pursuit: it helps one deal not only with the rough places, like quitting smoking, but also the holes and tangles of everyday living. After a fretful, fussy day, what is more relaxing, more satisfying, than the neat, steady click-click of needles knitting up, as Shakespeare puts it, "the raveled sleeve of care"? I seldom make holes and tangles in my sweaters any longer, and I believe, with the help of knitting, perhaps smaller holes and tangles in my life as well.

Never Idle

Janet Muench

My mother's hands were never idle. She tatted delicate lace edging for linen handkerchiefs, hooked colorful rugs, crocheted granny-square afghans, needlepointed beautiful pillows and chair covers, cross-stitched flowered quilts, and knitted complicated sweaters and delicate Barbie-doll clothes. She gave most of these things away to her lucky family and friends. In her 90s, while living in an assisted-living facility, she knitted tiny baby blankets for at-risk preemies in the Ohio State University Hospital intensive care unit. After breaking her second hip and contracting pneumonia, she needed full-time care and moved into a nursing home. She was confined to her bed. By then her hands were knobby with arthritis, and cataracts limited her vision. Crocheted dishcloths became her specialty. The nurses who cared for her and anyone who visited her went away with a colorful dishcloth made with variegated pastel cotton yarn. I watched my perfectionist mother's crocheted dishcloths grow into odd shapes as her condition deteriorated. She couldn't get out of bed or feed herself; her breathing was labored; and pills did not suppress her pain. But I was aware that her frantic crocheting was her way of holding herself together. I realized that when the crocheting stopped her death would soon follow. Sure enough, she died three days after her last attempt to crochet.

Through this experience, I learned the power of needlecraft in helping us get through difficult situations. A few years back during my recuperation from a difficult, painful foot surgery, I knit an intricate Fair Isle cardigan. Since I had to stay off my feet, the knitting occupied my mind and hands. In the same way, while I sat through the night beside my dying mother, my fingers were busy with needles and yarn. I too will probably die with worsted-weight yarn all around me and size eight needles in my hands!

Act of Hope, Act of Faith

Joanne Seiff

This morning I sat down to start a new knitting pattern, carefully balancing the needles and the threadlike yarn I'd chosen. I didn't just sit down, though; I sat down for a moment in a comfortable cushioned rocker that a friend recently gave me. Another friend helped me repair it, wash the cushion covers, coat the maple with lemon oil. Embraced in this chair that represents my friends' love and affection, I sat down to take a rest and to look at something "fiber-related." Then my 75-pound dog lay down for a rest—on my foot.

That was it. I was going to stay put. As I started the pattern, which was luckily within arm's reach, I thought about the trust that we knitters place in one another. Every time I start a new pattern, once more carefully balancing the double-pointed needles and yarn in the treacherous beginning, when the fabric of the knitting itself has not yet begun to hold the needles together, I take the plunge. A mixture of hope and faith convinces me that I can risk this strange beginning, learn this new technique and trust a fellow knitter's directions. With the dog on my foot and the needles within reach, I was off on this new adventure in knitting.

Of course, most non-needlecraft people think of knitting as the most staid form of recreation. Knitting, the domain of old ladies and dowdy women, creates endless misshapen sweaters and itchy socks. I am sure there is no need to describe the look people give me when I tell them I am a knitter, a spinner and even a dyer. They make all sorts of stupid, unkind jokes that I quietly withstand. They dig themselves deeper into their own embarrassment as they continue on, hoping to make me feel uncomfortable and show me the error of my ways. Actually though, knitting is just as much a risk-taking activity as learning a new sport or making music. Do you remember the awkward feeling of trying to learn to hold a bat or to understand the rules of football? I've never conquered the bicycle. I can't get on a bicycle without feeling that wibble-wobble of uncertainty and loss of control over gravity. A different rush comes from making music . . . you have to bear the first squawks and squeals as you practice, feeling stupid, until suddenly, one day, you step out onto a stage and your sax solo soars out, above your own level of expectation, into the heavens. You only get that adrenaline risk and joy after years of practice, as a saxophonist or as (yes) a knitter.

The pleasure gained by trusting what seems like an impossible set of directions—being willing to take the time and follow the risk—can result in some of the most beautiful needlecraft I have ever seen. The problem with those doubters who ridicule knitting is that they lack the perseverance needed to take the risk. Their hands never got over those first pangs of learning the stitches. They doubt the necessity of knitting in an industrial age. (Yet no one feels we should stop learning math in schools, just because we have calculators. . . .) They refuse to believe that if they just keep working on the simple movements, the stitches will learn to form themselves and magic can ensue.

I try, these days, to talk about my fiber-oriented hobbies in public. I am not embarrassed anymore about my love of knitting, spinning and the like. When I listen to someone who derides what I do, I am much better equipped now to ride out the storm. Sometimes I suggest counterpoints to their arguments, but mostly I ignore them. I concentrate on making complicated patterns in my knitting, or in imagining something even more exquisite in my head. This is because I have taken the risk of trusting a fellow knitter's pattern or creating my own many times now. I have taken the risk and found that I can trust my needlecraft friends entirely, and both function and art will spring from my fingers.

Never Say Die

Jennifer Colyer Smith

My aunt, Sally Kallop, came from a small town in New York. She grew up, fell in love, got married, had four children, managed to finish her education and become an elementary school teacher. She touched the heart of everyone who knew her. She was very active in her church and her community, helping out anyone she could. She was a gift from God to all of us, full of life and an inspiration to so many people.

Among Sally's many talents was knitting. Every holiday brought special gifts from my aunt. Knitting for nine nieces and nephews, nine grandchildren and so many other people in her life never seemed like a chore to her. She did it with pleasure in her heart and a smile on her face. She'd never forget your special days.

Sally first got breast cancer in the 1980s, but she didn't let it slow her down. She had a mastectomy and moved on with her life. But eleven years later the cancer came back, this time spread throughout her body. Though the prognosis was grim, Sally fought with everything in her tiny 5'2" body. She never gave up. Throughout her illness, she was still filling everyone's life around her with the special handknit gifts for which she was renowned.

Sally's sister Andrea (my mother) and her husband started raising sheep on their farm in he late 1980s, producing fine merino wool, and Sally become one of their best customers. One day, while visiting with Sally and her husband, Don, Andrea found a trunk in Sally's guest bedroom. It was full of unfinished knitting projects. Andrea, knowing that Sally's time was probably short, thought there was little likelihood that Sally would ever finish all those projects. Sally, on the other hand, was determined to finish the projects in that trunk before she died.

It was at Christmastime, her favorite time of year, that Sally finally succumbed to the cancer she had been fighting for so long. Even though she died on December 18th, each and every one of Sally's relatives got something handmade by her as a Christmas gift. We can still look at and feel and wear those wonderful things made by her own now-still hands.

It took some time before Andrea finally got up the nerve to walk up those steps of Sally's house to the guest bedroom where the trunk still sat at the end of the guest bed. It was hard for her to open it. She was expecting to have to empty the trunk, to take all her sister's projects home with her. But the trunk was empty. Sally had indeed finished all those knitting projects. With God's help a determined frail woman finished her projects just as she had said she would.

Sally spent many years as a dedicated wife, mother and teacher. But only in her death could she teach her ultimate lesson: put your mind to something, and who knows? It may get done.

My Purple Sweater

Faye Whyte

My parents didn't have the money to buy a closet full of brand-name clothes for their teenage daughters, but my mother always took the time to fashion warm sweaters for us. We never lacked for handmade socks or mittens. She would tell us that the kids wearing the latest style were jealous that someone loved us enough to make handmade clothes for us. Of course I didn't believe her. At the time, I felt poor. The kids at my high school, although they had the latest labels on their backs, rarely wore handmade clothes. They wore brand-name clothes and created their own styles. One girl in particular, Alexandra, loved purple. She wore purple eye shadow, purple socks and purple earrings. She even had a pair of purple eyeglasses. She wore all the latest fashions, in shades of purple.

One day when I complained about my lack of new school clothes, my mother said to me, in the practical tones of the adult, "Why not make some new clothes?" What a concept! I had been knitting since age five. My completed projects to date consisted mostly of potholders, socks and gloves. Why not make a sweater?

Mom got out her knitting books and I pored through them until I spotted the perfect sweater: a cardigan with cables, bobbles and set-in, puffed sleeves. It was breathtaking. It never occurred to me that the pattern would be a challenge even for an experienced knitter, and my mother was kind enough not to mention that fact. We set out that fall day for the local yarn store. I had never selected yarn for a project before—and I must say the thrill is still the same. I don't know how my mother put up with me that afternoon. First, we had to consult with the proprietor about all possible yarns that would be appropriate for my project. I made a list and set a ball of each onto the counter. Then I had to choose a color.

I knew it would be purple. Not too light, like lilac or mauve. Not too blue. Not too bright. I thought and grinned and vacillated until I had chosen the perfect shade of eggplant. Twelve balls, please. Mind the lot number. Before we arrived home, I had started the first ball from the inside, as Mom always did.

For the next two months, my family knew where to find me in my spare time. I would be planted on the couch, hunched over the pattern book, wrestling with my needles and trying not to swear. Aside from the difficulty of the pattern itself, I'm a left-handed knitter who learned from a right-handed knitter. I never figured out how to hold the needles properly, so I knit with one needle jammed against my thigh and the other whipping though the air. To watch my technique, you would think I couldn't keep an even tension. When I started that sweater, I couldn't, but I learned. My other challenge was a streak of stubborn perfectionism. Each time I would get two or three inches of the pattern started, if a dropped stitch couldn't be salvaged or the tension in the cable wasn't just right, I would mercilessly tear the whole garment out and start again. When she saw me huff and slide the needles free, my mother would leave the room. To this day, she can't bear to see me tear something out.

Finally, I had all the pieces finished and I began painstakingly to sew them together. The sewing took another two weeks. The puffed sleeves on that sweater were my first and last. By spring the new sweater was almost ready to wear. I skipped the part where all the little ends are sewn in; I only darned the ones that might be seen from the outside. I also hadn't chosen buttons yet, but I couldn't wait any longer. I had to show it off at school.

My purple sweater was a hit. It was the finest garment at the school. I puffed up with pride each time I told someone, "I made it myself." Some of the kids didn't believe me, but that didn't matter. Everyone was impressed with my beautiful sweater, even Alexandra. I wore it as often as I dared, usually once or twice a week. Mom got me a white blouse to wear under it that set off the intricate knit pattern. I was so proud of that sweater. Some of the girls even borrowed it, including Alexandra.

I never got the chance to sew buttons onto my purple sweater. One day—it may have been at the end of a school day or after a dance, I can't remember—I couldn't find it. It was suddenly gone. I checked all my drawers and my closet. I searched the car and my locker and every inch of my classroom. I tore my sister's room apart and staked out the laundry room for days. I cried, I yelled, I suspected everyone I knew of stealing my beautiful purple sweater.

The sweater never surfaced. It's been years and I've made dozens of sweaters since then. But I will never forget my purple sweater, my first. On quiet evenings, when the family is settled and I'm sitting in my favorite armchair knitting something for my daughter, I think of that sweater. And, although I'll never know for sure, I have to think my mother was right all along. That sweater made me rich, in a way, because someone out there, some girl like Alexandra with lots of nice store-bought clothes, was so moved by my handmade sweater that she had to have it. I hope she loved it as much as I did.

Addictions

Kirsten Ossorio

I came by my compulsive knitting honestly, albeit the hard way. First, there was the compulsion to drink, which, because I could always sustain that socially desirable condition we call "high-functioning," accompanied me all the way through my twenties. When I was thirty I had had enough: I substituted compulsive self-examination for compulsive drinking. At Alcoholics Anonymous meetings I examined why I drank the way I drank for as long as I drank. I explored the implications of my having mixed vodka with Valium: was I not just an alcoholic, but also a drug addict? Almost everything anyone said at AA meetings was grist for my compulsive self-examination mill. I identified with the stories of misunderstood artistry told by AA members who had also been street-drug users—people who stuck hypodermic needles in their arms, some of them apparently the size of European #1 knitting needles. These stories felt so familiar to me that I wondered whether I wasn't maybe an all-purpose addict.

After a couple of years I became thoroughly bored with self-examination as I took up knitting. I'm certain there was a causal relationship: the knitting so calmed my frenetically analyzing mind that the intellectual channels of my self-scrutiny were significantly narrowed, and occasionally entirely blocked. Knitting let me hear what people were saying for what it was, and take people in for who they were. It tamped down my ego and tuned me in to the reality around me. Knitting helped me take in people's tones of voice, their words, and their intentions. Knitting dissolved much of my pressing, self-centered need to analyze everything about and around me.

I would be less than honest if I failed to acknowledge that I am now a compulsive knitter. True, I rarely knit except at AA meetings. But it's also true that I almost *always* knit at AA meetings. I seem to *need* to knit at AA meetings. I've been known, en route to an AA meeting, to turn my car around and go home to fetch my knitting. I'd rather arrive late than sit there empty-handed, deprived of my yarn fix. I can tell how many meetings I go to by how quickly I'm progressing with my latest sweater.

I fear that my compulsive need to knit may be a progressive condition. In fact, I see that in my compulsion, I have just lied about the extent of my knitting habit. Probably I am in knitting-compulsion denial. It is not the case, as I just stated, that I rarely knit except at AA meetings. To tell the truth, recently my sweetie and I got a big-screen TV and a DVD player, and now I spend several hours a week knitting in front of a movie in our living room.

Not surprisingly, my compulsion/addiction is becoming increasingly expensive, which is frighteningly typical of the progression of alcohol and drug addictions. My yarn expenditures have risen as a result of my putting in more hours with the needles, and I am now forced to consider ameliorative measures. Maybe I'll switch to smaller needles, thinner yarns, or more synthetics. Perhaps I could share needles.

Compulsive or not, my knitting is also a form of meditation. Knitting is even, like my breathing when I meditate. When knitting I count stitches, as, when meditating, I count my breaths. And knitting has it all over meditation in at least one immensely gratifying regard: it results in a tangible, desirable, short-term outcome that I can wear.

Also, knitting is a marvelous judgment filter. A guy named Percy once asked me at an AA meeting if I could really be present for the business at hand while I was concentrated on my knitting. He was obviously not a knitter. He probably thought that knitting requires detailed attention at every moment, rather than allowing me to rest, focus, and be all the more present at AA meetings. I told Percy that when I'm not knitting at AA meetings I'm easily annoyed by comments that I find especially simplistic, illogical, or self-delusional. When I'm not knitting, I become sidetracked by irritation when people launch into lengthy, laborious lectures on AA's history, or when some long-sober pillar of the AA community tells other people how they should live their lives (rare, but not unheard of). Percy looked skeptical when I explained that knitting adjusts my brain waves into a pattern that acts as a filter, preventing such aggravations from penetrating fully. But how could Percy know? Other knitters understand.

Aside from being a form of meditation and a method of blocking out the more irritating people and comments in AA, knitting acts as a sort of euphoric. That's right: it's a bit of a drug. Sometimes when I'm knitting at AA meetings I tune out my judgmental nature so completely that I can actually feel the endorphins releasing in my brain. It's almost like getting high. Apparently this semi-euphoria is evident not only to me, on the basis of what it feels like, but to others, who can see what it looks like. For instance, one day when I was knitting my way toward a semi-high, working on the second sleeve of a sea-green V-neck in a linen stitch, my AA friend Elia whispered, humorously, "Earth to Kirsten." Did Elia, who had some experience with that other kind of needle, find something familiar about my quasi-euphoric state? Just as he was whispering to me I began to laugh at something the AA speaker had just said. She was talking about switching from a heroin addiction to a milder addiction to cigarettes and, more recently, to a serious fruit juice habit. As she put it, "From needles, to nicotine, to Nantucket Nectars." Everyone in the room was laughing, perhaps because we were all reminded of the many compulsive phases we'd gone through since we had become sober and clean. I was also wondering idly just how compulsive my knitting really was.

At that moment Elia looked down at my knitting, shifted his gaze meaningfully to the two women opposite us who were also knitting, and said quietly, smilingly, slightly wistfully: "Better be careful, dear; you know: addicts and their needles."

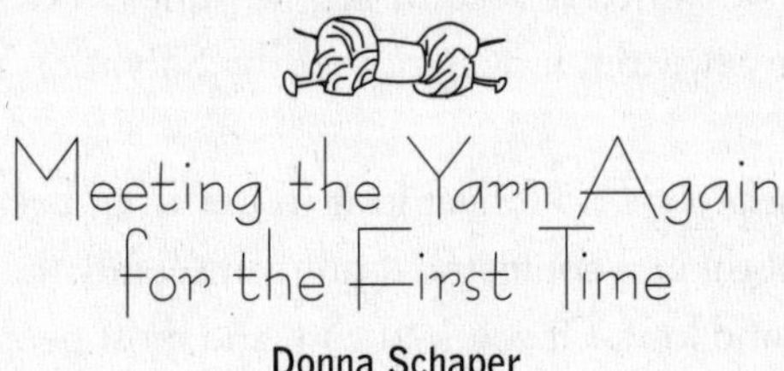

Meeting the Yarn Again for the First Time

Donna Schaper

I knit during meetings. Or rather, I used to knit during meetings. Now I remember the times I used to knit during meetings—and remember these times, nostalgically, as a simpler time. Then I was multi-tasking the meeting, doing two things at once, sometimes writing poems and grocery lists in the margin of my notebook while seeming to take prodigious notes on the substance of the session. Or I would appear to pay serious attention to the meeting's profundities while knitting, purling and counting stitches. I finished many a scarf and quilt (I call them quilts; others call them afghans) in these settings. I even attempted a sweater or two. The sweaters all came out lopsided; I couldn't really fake attention while counting stitches. Consequently, I probably had a couple of years of very bad meeting attention while ruining quite a bit of yarn. Neither of these things mattered that much.

Failing to complete the sweaters was more serious a loss but not that bad as to cause serious grief. Sweaters can be bought at the Salvation Army store for a couple of dollars, and many of them are quite fine. What I lost with the lopsided sweaters was the sense of pride in having made them myself. When people complimented these sweaters that never were, I could have quietly said, "I made it myself." Demurely. Without showing the pride I felt inside. These conceits were never to be: I am condemned to second-degree pride; when people say they like my sweater, I say I got it at the Salvation Army for a song.

Unfortunately, I no longer knit in meetings because I now run most of them. People find it quite unseemly that I can run a meeting and knit. Of course, I can, and most people can, especially women, but there are certain things you don't want to let people know you can do. It's too "in their face." Golda Meir is said to have said, more than once, "I can type but don't tell anyone." I understand her discretion. Double-timing a meeting can be as dangerous as double-timing a husband, if the wrong people take notice.

Thus, to knit at this stage in my life, I would have to knit during free time, unencumbered time, as genuine leisure. While I like knitting, I don't like it enough to impose upon it the sacredness of Sabbath. I also need almost all my free time to exercise and not sit, given how important I have become and how important people think my meetings are. The meetings are not that important but people think they are. Likewise my sweater loss was not that important but I thought it was, for a long time. I lost things inside the loss of the sweater—and these do command my complete attention.

I can no longer buy yarn with impunity. I just moved out of a house that I had lived in for seven good years, and I had to give away a lot of unknit yarn. It was very painful. Some of it was so beautiful that it had to be given away to exactly the right person, and I couldn't find her. She wasn't there. I have known some good knitters in my life, people who could have used the fluffy light blue (only three skeins), the rayon-based multi-colored of which I had tons left, the white angora that I bought at a yard sale in Shelburne Falls, a place that still has real sheep. But all these people had given up knitting too. One was in California running the French department at a large university; she told me she "doesn't knit anymore." I couldn't bear to find out why. Another is with a new lover and "doesn't even think about knitting anymore."

My French professor friend always had the best basket in the corner of her study, filled with yarn so warm that you wanted to turn yourself into a cat and sit in it. Hers did, with impunity. My in-love friend joined my California friend in making stunning sweaters. They caused me great envy.

I ended up taking the yarn to the Salvation Army and to my dismay it was still there, with a lot of other lonely yarn balls, the next week, right before I moved away. The misfit yarn basket at the Salvation Army could have broken my heart that day if I hadn't bought a sweater.

The loss of my yarn, some of which I had bought second-hand, really disturbed me. I wasn't just throwing away thread. I was throwing away the old me, now condemned to unimportance as I am condemned to importance.

Mid-term in my season of importance, I ran into some very fine yarns, just as orphaned and misfitted as those I had left behind in the move. The yarns were at the Jewish Recycling Center in North Miami, one of the fine thrift shops in my new area. There was enough for a small quilt, a hodgepodge to be sure, but a small quilt nonetheless. I bought the yarns, and they sit in a basket in my study, waiting to be caressed and turned and twisted into togetherness. One of my goals is not to leave this season of importance without an unimportant quilt made.

I hate unknit yarn. Unknit yarn means that something that could have been connected is isolated. It reminds me of what

I have left behind: a simpler complexity, a double-timing and a multi-tasking that now looks simple compared to the web and knots I face daily. Now, in meetings, while running them, I don't have time even for the silly poems and the grocery lists. Instead, I am often caught writing memos to assistants while appearing to listen to other assistants. A strange webbed and tangled world it is. I happen to like it very much. I like knitting the people to each other and to their task. But it is not as simple as a quilt or scarf. It is nearer the challenge of a sweater—and more and more things do appear to come out lopsided. More and more also come out beautifully—and that of course is what keeps me hurling my second- and thirdhand fragments at a potential unity.

I am told that E. B. White thought of the purpose of writing as that of untangling the English language. I think of the purpose of knitting as tangling. Artful tangling but tangling nonetheless. I wouldn't want to go so far as to say that I am still knitting, even that I am still mourning knitting. But I do have a quilt that might yet be made. That will have to do for me.

Winter Things

Lucinda J. Garthwaite

At 7:30 in the morning on her forty-ninth birthday, Kathryn Windham wiped the counter with the red and yellow dishcloth she'd pulled from the laundry that morning. She'd had her usual bowl of cereal with raisins; she'd swallowed her vitamins with three small gulps of grape juice; she'd rinsed her bowl and screwed the caps on all the vitamin jars. She'd read the front page of the local paper and folded it on the kitchen table, to finish reading at the end of her day.

She didn't notice the rat droppings until she'd rolled several into the folds of the damp rag. When the third or fourth pushed up against her fingertip through the rag, she stopped and turned the rag over to inspect it. She thought first of dill seeds, then quickly dismissed the idea—too big. She stood looking for a full ten seconds before her face crumpled. She dropped the rag, and jumped back from the counter, looking instinctively down at her feet, as if the rat might that second run across them. Lifting one foot, then another, still grimacing, she pulled her shoulders up around her neck and fled the kitchen, the rag balled up on the counter where she'd left it.

She stopped in the doorway by the hall phone, thinking to call her daughter Rachel, but only stood then, her hand resting on the back of the receiver, leaning her forehead on the door frame. She couldn't think about the rats. She would return to sorting through her husband's clothes. Rachel had come last week to help, and they'd finished the closet, the dresser, the workbench. Rachel took some things; others they'd tossed out or boxed for Goodwill. Rachel laughed over the golf balls, each labeled with the date of play and shots over or under par, that Kathryn's husband had stuffed into socks at the back of the top dresser drawer. Kathryn weighed one of the odd sacks on one hand, an unpaired wool sock full at the toe with four or five golf balls. She saw there were more of them shoved away like stolen money there in the drawer she'd never opened before. She looked up to Rachel, saw instead herself in the mirror, frowning, and set the sock down. Rachel didn't notice, and reached into the drawer to pull out the rest.

"Do you want to save these, Mom?"

Kathryn shook her head, recovering herself. "No. You have them if you want them. He'd like it if you had them." Rachel looked in the sacks at the dates, kept the most recent, and threw the others away.

Today Kathryn would tackle the winter things, things she

had stored two months ago in March, in a new plastic tub marked "Sweaters, wool socks, winter misc." Tonight Rachel would come to take her out to dinner and would take the Goodwill boxes away.

But at the moment there were the rats to worry about. Kathryn had never trapped a rat herself, nor had she drowned any, as her husband had one spring when he found a nest in the pile of tarps he kept for the woodpile. She remembered watching him fill the bucket, hearing the silence as he waited for the rats to drown and then the deep swish as he tossed water and dead rats in back of the shed. She'd asked him not to drown them, had suggested instead that he leave them be, out there. "Let the cats have their way with them," she'd said. But he'd kept filling the bucket. "You want rats in the house?" he'd asked, and walked out the back door without waiting for an answer.

Kathryn linked her hands behind her neck and pulled against it, took a breath and let it out hard as she stepped back into the kitchen. She guessed if there were rats, there'd be more droppings in the cupboards under the counter and sink, so she set about opening each one, determined at least to clean up after them. She stood to the side of the first cupboard door and pulled it open, peering in from behind and over the door, with her head pulled back, half expecting a rat to jump from the top of a pot. The cupboard under the sink was full of buckets, a compost jar, and cleaning rags, in a messy pile on the bottom of the cupboard. In the center of the rag pile were six tiny pink baby rats, asleep.

Kathryn didn't move at first. She reached for the drawer over her left shoulder and pulled it open, took from it a flashlight that, without looking, she knew would be there, and shined the light on the sleeping baby rats. Then, in a momentary panic, she shined the light around the rest of the cupboard, looking for the parents. Nothing moved in the cupboard, except the quick breath of the babies. The handful of babies slept curled against each other with backsides and heads either on or off the pile. While Kathryn watched, one slid off completely in its sleep, and paddled with its tiny legs to push itself back toward the center.

There were two buckets set one inside the other in the cupboard under the sink. Kathryn imagined holding one at the edge of the cupboard, using a dustpan, maybe, to slide the sleeping rat babies into the bucket to bring outside, maybe to the shed, she thought, and dump them all into a corner there. Then she thought maybe just the dustpan; she'd push them onto it with the dust broom, or into a box. She could close a box, she thought, and get out to the shed. She worried, though, that they might wake while she carried them, gnaw at the box, and get out and onto her arms. She had a vague understanding that rats were dangerous. She didn't think baby rats could be vicious, but rabid, perhaps, or otherwise diseased.

Then she thought of the winter things, of the big plastic tub they were in with the lid that clicked into place and held. She was sure they couldn't gnaw through that in the time it would take to get them to the shed. She shut the cupboard doors, set the light on the counter, and went upstairs.

The plastic tub was clear enough to show the colors of its contents. As she pulled it down from the attic, she saw the layers of burgundy, blue, black, and tan that marked her husband's things. Most of them she'd made herself. She'd chosen wool in colors he would wear, and knitted simple, sturdy patterns. She set the tub on the floor in the hallway, lifted the lid, and sat cross-legged there to empty it. Each sweater she pulled out and held by the shoulders, looking for moth holes automatically; each year of their marriage she'd done this, examined all their winter things for holes. Each year there was a sock, sometimes a sweater, past darning, that she'd throw away. She was looking for one of those now, she realized, looking for something to line the bottom of the tub for the babies under the kitchen sink.

The first sweater was a blue crew neck, not the first she'd knitted for him, but like it except for color. Before they were married, for his birthday, she'd done a red one. She'd been living at home with her parents then, sharing the small house they'd always had. She knitted the red sweater in the mornings before her parents were up, hurrying to gather the ball of yarn from the floor before her father stumbled in and tripped on it. She hadn't developed the habit then, yet, of leaving the yarn in a bag. Two years later, her husband had made her a gift of a cedar box with brass hinges and a round hole at the top. He'd presented it to her with three balls of cheap acrylic blue yarn stacked neatly inside, a single strand weaving out of the top. The card attached read, "Knit me another in blue, will you?" She loved the box, and had knitted him the sweater she held now, of yarn that had outlasted later sweaters made of finer stuff. She took out another and another, both whole, and folded them neatly on top of the blue crew neck.

She came then to the layer of socks, slid one onto her hand to turn it back and forth to look it over. It was of gray wool speckled with brown. She liked the feel of the wool on her fingers. The yarn was undyed, from a particular sheep (she remembered now) on a farm she'd found when she was knitting often. With her palm turned toward her, she bent her fingers to look at the toes, and smiled at the memory of Rachel using the socks as puppets. "Will I do for the rat bed?" Kathryn spoke for the sock, wiggling her fingers with each word. "No, Mr. Sock, you're too healthy. Back in the box you go." She caught herself welling up, then wiped her eyes with the sock and pulled it off her hand, pairing it with its mate with a quick twist and tuck.

Kathryn hadn't progressed much, as a knitter, since she'd first taught herself how as a teenager. It had been for the quiet, mostly, that she'd learned. Her parents' house was loud with anger or thick silence—mostly in response to, or to keep a lid on, her father's drinking. She'd read a lot as a child, alone in her bedroom, lying very still, buried in a story. But when she got older her mother began to call her lazy. "Do something, for God's sake," she'd say, standing in the doorway of Kathryn's bedroom. So Kathryn took up knitting, which seemed to fit her mother's definition of "doing something" more than reading did.

She'd knitted scarves first, for each of her parents, and sat relieved and happy at how pleased they were when she presented them. Her mother even said to her father, "Well, look at this," and they'd smiled at each other. The occasion of each gift to her parents of something she'd made meant a break from the tension in the house. She'd learned to hold on to her knitted things, to offer them just when her mother was most silent or her father about to explode. She offered them more scarves, then hats as she learned how to hold the tension in her knitting, finally squaring the edges of her scarves.

But the first sweater she made was for her husband—her boyfriend then. She married him a year later, at eighteen, grateful for his quiet voice and for his attention. Three years after that, Rachel came. Kathryn knitted booties, too many, while she was pregnant, and a tiny yellow sweater the baby wore only once, crying the whole time from the itch of it. Once Rachel was born Kathryn was too overwhelmed to knit, and two miscarriages after that she was too sad. She shopped at department stores for sweaters and hats, busied herself with keeping the house and Rachel calm. If her husband was sad, she didn't know it, though she imagined he might be sad or angry as they spoke less, took less time with each other, and turned their lives to Rachel.

Only when Rachel asked for a ski sweater like the ones her friends were wearing did Kathryn start knitting again. She knitted the sweater for Rachel and another for her husband that year, starting in late September on Rachel's orange and yellow stripes. She'd been so long away from it then that she unraveled each sleeve twice, slid the loops off of the needles, pulled until she found the place she'd started to lose the pattern, started the count again. By mid-November, she had practiced enough on Rachel's to get her husband's right. He liked it well enough, she thought then, watching him hold it up to himself and model it next to Rachel. Then he put it aside, laughing at Rachel's pretending to ski in hers. She wondered then if the sweater was too bulky, the burgundy color too close to purple for him to wear.

That had been Rachel's last year of high school. Once she left home, Kathryn sat reading most evenings, waiting for her husband to get home, often late. They ate quietly, sat and chatted about Rachel with each other. He spoke to Rachel most days from his office, as Kathryn did most days from home. If he didn't go out after dinner, he'd putter in the workroom while she cleaned up and read. It hadn't seemed like such a bad life to her, though occasionally she'd realize how young they really were, and wondered what she might do with herself, now that Rachel was grown. She hadn't expected the crash from the workroom, or the ambulance or the hospital chaplain explaining her husband hadn't survived. She hadn't expected the depth of the silence that followed.

She held that burgundy sweater up now, lifted the shoulders to look it over, and saw that this one had holes under each arm, worn holes, not moths. The yarn had pulled away from the seams, leaving uneven strands of yarn. She realized he had worn it, then. It was stretched out at the waist, his paunch grown under it in the twelve years since she'd given it to him. She set it aside, unfolded, then picked it up and folded it onto the pile with the others. There were more sweaters, a few hats, and socks to sort—which she did, making a considerable pile to save, leaving several out she thought she'd throw away. She'd forgotten the rats for a time, but when she remembered them, she dropped the throwaway pile in the tub and carried it downstairs.

She opened the cupboard door again, carefully, and was relieved to see them still sleeping. She set the tub down on its side against the edge of the cupboard and put the top within easy reach. With a broom, she reached to the back of the pile of rags and pushed the whole thing into the tub. The rats woke then, started to squeak the tiniest of sounds, and Kathryn quickly righted the tub and popped on the top, hitting it with the heel of her hand to lock it shut. She stepped back and waited, wondered what she would do if a mother or father rat responded to the squeaking babies, but no adult rat appeared. The babies settled down, burrowing into the ruined winter things to sleep again. Kathryn carried them out to the shed, lifted the lid and watched for a moment, and left the tub where it was.

Back in the house, she pulled the burgundy sweater off the pile again, and stacked the rest in boxes for Rachel later. She stood and stretched, then went to a closet and pulled out a grocery bag of leftover yarn. With her free hand, she rooted around in the bag, looking for something that nearly matched the sweater she held. Finding none, she pulled out the top ball of yarn, and sat down to mend the holes.

The Gray Shawl

Nancy W. Hall

I knew something was wrong when I packed for a vacation that involved a lot of car time and didn't take my knitting. My husband cocked an eyebrow at my empty hands as I sat beside him in the front seat, and asked, "What? No yarn?" I could only shrug. "I'm just taking a little break," I answered lightly, but the truth scared me: I didn't want to knit anymore. Didn't even *want* to want to.

For twenty years knitting has been my art form, my meditation, my solace in sorrow, my celebration in times of joy. My kids are used to hearing, "As soon as I finish this row." My family obligingly plans vacations around promising yarn shops. I knit in classes, in meetings, even in my sleep, my hands continuing their rhythmic work as my eyes drift shut during a dull movie or television program. So of course I packed my knitting after getting the call: my father had cancer, and I needed to come home—now. Knitting kept me calm on that plane trip, each stitch of a gray wool shawl soothing and predictable. Imperceptibly, the shawl grew as I flew toward my dying father.

Many times that summer and fall, I knitted from Connecticut to Tennessee and back again. I knitted in my parents' den, knitted as Dad chatted on strong days or dozed when the chemotherapy sapped his strength. I knitted in emergency rooms in the middle of the night, in oncology ward lounges, by his bedside in the hospital. Finally, I knitted my way through the afternoon of Dad's funeral, as my sister and I sat among the coffee cups and half-eaten sandwiches and cakes and my mother slept for the first time in days. That December evening I finished the shawl, stuffing it unceremoniously into my suitcase. I read on the flight home.

And now I couldn't knit at all. I couldn't face finishing my intricate blue and white socks, my cashmere cap, my son's pullover. Even browsing through my yarn stash, which had always brought me such inspiration and comfort, had lost its charm. Stroking shimmering skeins of hand-painted silk yarns or fat balls of jewel-colored wools failed to pique my interest. What was happening? Knitting friends brought the answer to which I had been blind. Your knitting is associated with your dad's death, they said. It will take time to unravel the knitting from your grief and loss. They gently shared their own stories of knitting at the bedsides of sick and dying friends and relatives, and of being unable for months or even years afterward to be soothed or sparked by the cottony or woolen or silken threads that had previously been so tightly knit with happier memories. Let it be for a while, they urged. Read, play, be with your family, be patient.

Recently I dampened and smoothed that gray shawl into shape, each stitch worked with love and concern for my father. I straightened each repeat of the pattern, remembering the too-short life of the good man who had so valued his own creative outlets, his paintings and carvings and woodcuts, his big blue earthenware bowls full of fragrantly rising bread dough. As I smoothed a bumpy row here, evened a lacy bit there, I could almost feel the knitting needles in my hands, familiar and yet challenging. Carrying the finished shawl to the closet, I passed my shelves of knitting books, their covers gathering dust but their plans for tapestry-rich mittens, whimsical children's sweaters and traditional lacy scarves faintly beckoning.

I may still not want to knit, but I'm beginning to want to want to knit. And when I sit down again to create something soft and warm and beautiful, I know the memory of my father will be wrapped into every stitch.

After James Died

Harry Kelley

After James died there were the sweaters. There was a blue vest that I began to wear. There was the red-ribbed pullover in sports weight, very fashionable, very handsome. There was a profoundly complicated Fair Isle. Actually, the Fair Isle had been Richard's. I actually lied once when someone asked about it and said that I had knit it. I couldn't explain that Richard is dead. I couldn't say, Well, my partner Richard knit it, and he's dead, and now I'm wearing it. Well, I could have, but I just couldn't right then, right there. I couldn't explain about the blue vest either.

The blue vest has a cable, one, up the middle of the front to a nice handsome V. The yarn is masculine, a rich blue, not too far from denim. It has flecks of beige. For a long time wearing the vest was a way of keeping James nearby. But the other day, I found it on the floor. It's been 12 years since James died. You think after 12 years that the feeling changes somehow. But the stars don't change and the seasons don't change. No, time doesn't heal all wounds; that's not how it works. Rather, wounds heal time—you suddenly find, after the hard work of grief, that this hard thing has made you take the hard step and you have grown. You may look more contorted, more wrinkled, more bent, more scarred. But inside the heart beats with a deeper tattoo. Grief does not depart—don't let anyone ever convince you that it does. When you learned to walk, didn't you fall? Didn't it hurt? Didn't you cry? Your legs didn't go away though. And grief, which gives the soul perambulation, doesn't end. The grief gives you a way to journey. It allows you to walk, to fly, to purchase new horizons, to see new worlds, to listen more attentively.

Jim—the one who is alive, with whom I live now—knits too. I taught him. It was easy. Jim was a dancer. He made a career in the ballet. He studied at School of American Ballet and danced with City Ballet, New York State Theatre, and a host of regional companies where he would dance the Prince in *The Nutcracker*. Within three minutes of my starting to teach him how to knit, he cried out, "Oh, I get it!" "What?" I was irritated and incredulous. "There are two steps in dancing. There are two steps in knitting. Forward, backward, knit, purl." And he was knitting well within ten minutes. It was delightful and infuriating. His first project was a three-colored cardigan. Buttonholes. Capped sleeves. He made it for me.

It may be hard for you to fathom, unless you have lost everything over a few times. But I wasn't happy to have a sweater knit for me. I felt numb. How unwilling, how afraid I was, to let fragile and vibrant life happen in me, to *me*. How awful I was in that moment, unable to feel gratitude or express astonishment when Jim gave me the sweater. It was the first sweater anyone had knit for me. I was afraid of it. I was afraid of finding it in my drawer, carefully folded, after Jim died someday. I was afraid too of green plants, because they can die. I wouldn't have a dog or cat because a dog or a cat can languish and die, or be hit by a car and die. And I was afraid that the sweater would survive Jim one day, and the sweater and I would be trapped in a room somewhere unable to talk about him. I didn't want to feel too happy about this moment, about this life, because I was afraid of how it might stab in my heart when I lost it.

I helped stitch the AIDS quilt. In fact I had been there showing people how to stitch the first squares together. I had appliquéed a square for James: in it, he is lying in bed, dead, with the moon outside his window, the cats on a chair looking at him. I tried to put in the subtle fleeting serenity that calmed me as I read him the 18th Psalm. (Why did I pick that one? Except that I felt such gratitude for the sky in that moment of his dying.) When I was making the square for James someone said, "Relax, it isn't like you're trying to win a contest." And I responded, "No, but this will hang in the Smithsonian one day." I was guessing, of course, but I hear it will hang in the Smithsonian when it comes to rest. And I was stunned when my work filled an entire movie screen for a few seconds in the Oscar-winning documentary about the making of the AIDS quilt.

I did not know how the sweaters too would become a vast plane. They are a tribute to grief, loneliness, and lost richness. They are creatures. They live the lives of solitary, lonely beasts. Every stitch, you know—every stitch—like every cell in a leaf, in an eye, in the blood circulating, in the heart—like every thought in a day, is crafted by the hand of tender abundance, and poured from the Heart of Compassion. But like creatures, sweaters age, they harden, they slowly lose their stitched purchase. The sweaters do not know who made them.

They help me sometimes. By letting my grief pour without meaning, by letting me grieve without working at grieving. By not demanding poetry. By lacking nostalgic sentiments. By making no demands. They curl up in the drawer and hide from the light. They unfurl themselves and consent to appear in restaurants, in church, at work, boldly defending their owner-by-happenstance. But they feel no need to tell the story of how they lost their owners and went on. Even as they age a bit, stretch a bit, pill a bit. Even as I must tell over and over the stories of what happened.

When you are a man and you knit and people see you, sooner or later someone is compelled to come up and say, "You know, King Frederick knit!" I always respond, "Isn't that curious? Because so did my grandmother." Meaning of course that I knit because my grandmother taught me, but also that she is the one I think of, and that I don't really need any model but her. Granny taught me when I was six. Richard knit too. And James. And now Jim knits.

I do not have a drawer full of beautiful sweaters that tell the story of a life. Like so many knitters before me, I have never knit a sweater for myself. I have a blue vest I let fall on the floor. And a red pullover that is too small for me. And a beautiful blue cardigan with intricate color design and silver buttons. And I have a million knitting needles, all of them left over, like bones. The needles are precious to me. I wear when I can these knots of history, the colors of last year and the year before, the hand of the past. But the needles are eternal. Bone or birch, they point forward. Some are clearly old. But all point forward.

Plying the Spirit

Wild Harvesting

Luisa Gelenter

Ah, so it's Kota gathering time again. Standing in this never-plowed glorious high mountain meadow in New Mexico, I remember why I got into this plant-dyeing business in the first place. It gives me a reason to do one of the things I love best: tramp around in high country. As a plant dyer, I have the excuse of being "on the hunt" for dye plants. So I get to do my job surrounded by big ever-changing skies and mountain vistas and kindred company. Well, it's my job and I *am* working!

Saturday night. I can't fall asleep for wondering how could it be that in this year of unbearable drought and horrible forest fires, my most special native dye plant, Kota, is so abundant. We had a drought last year and the Kota was terribly sparse. This year the drought is worse. I need a botanist/herbalist with a specialty in the native plants of northern New Mexico to explain this to me, but where would I find such a person?

Sunday morning. It's 7 A.M. and the crew shows up for the drive to the Mora area and the Kota harvest. This is pure field-hand work, stoop labor, but we often have the most amazing people show up to help. I believe that it's due somewhat to our collective memory from our hunting and gathering days. I think that for some (of whom I'm one), it gives deep and ancient satisfaction to be harvesting these wild fruits of the Earth. I have had all kinds of crews along on these wild harvests, from gonzo teenage boys to PhDs to people from the Taos Pueblo—anyone able-bodied I can rope into going along. But today's crew is especially spectacular. Among the amazing folks at my door on this beautiful blue-eyed July morning are my two dye assistants, an organic gardener, a Chinese mathematician who works at the Los Alamos labs, a metal sculptor and—lo and behold!—my prayed-for botanist/herbalist. This is pure magic, since I had never met him before. I ask him ALL my questions and he answers them fully. It is so wonderful, as we harvest Kota in these high-altitude mountain meadows. He identifies all the flowers in the field and tells me about their medicinal uses and survival tricks. Abundant blooming in the second drought year is one such trick. If the Kota don't put out herculean efforts this second year of drought season, they will die out. Hence their abundance in this terrible year.

There must be the cure for almost anything in these meadows, I suspect, just like as the Amazon rain forest—treatments for cancer, AIDS, all the ills that plague us. I dream about buying a few acres of one of these meadows just to walk in year after year, never to plow or to build on. My own little land trust. Dream on, Luisa!

After we gather these plants we shape them into a bagel-like form for drying and saving in a "package" that will fit in the dye pots. We then dye all our yarn lines with the colors that Kota can give us. Then it's up to the knitters!

Knitting as Spiritual Practice

Catherine Hinard

I find it intriguing that almost every knitter I know loves to knit, loves to be making something but hates to finish it. Whether or not we actually produce something is often beside the point. It's the very act of knitting that we love. We know the value of picking up the yarn and the needles and sitting down to work on our craft. Through our knitting, we can be transported into an exciting, sensual world filled with color and texture and with the thrill of something growing and unfolding in our hands. We love the way in which knitting fosters patience in us and can reduce our stress.

We knit in meetings, in waiting rooms, at airports; I even knit in the car while stuck in traffic or at red lights. We knit to stay sane. Knitters find great satisfaction in the neatness of knitting, the organization of the stitches and the rows, the sense of something fitting together so perfectly and progressing along so methodically. I believe knitters instinctively recognize that knitting is far more than the construction of a finished garment—rather, it is a therapeutic endeavor that can be an actual meditation practice.

In the crazy pace of contemporary society, we turn to knitting to slow us down and to relax us. We are calmed and lulled by the soothing, almost hypnotic click of our needles. The captivating rhythm of knitting gives us a chance to step back and view our lives from a little bit of a distance. Our passion for the craft allows us to set aside our endless "to do" lists and just sit, relishing an orderly calm. Through knitting, we achieve a state of peace, a sense of spaciousness not requiring thought. It can be very freeing. At the same time, we are engaged in a specific task that can involve an intense focus. This focus can bring us into the moment, allowing the "internal dialogue," the mind's seemingly endless chatter, to quiet down. As a result, knitting grounds us in stillness.

Meditation also grounds us in stillness. The practice of meditation requires patience, a willingness simply to allow life to happen while we sit in stillness quietly watching what spontaneously arises. Knitting, too, requires patience, a willingness to let creation happen leisurely, to wait and to see what emerges. Both knitting and meditation lend us a profound experience of concentration that can help us release anxiety and find serenity.

Concentration is an integral part of meditation, and as knitters, we are already experts in concentration. In traditional meditation practice, we are taught to follow the breath, to use the breath as our point of concentration, again and again returning to the breath when we find ourselves becoming distracted and caught up in thought. Knitting functions as a meditation tool when we use the fashioning of each stitch as our point of concentration. If we find ourselves distracted and caught up in thinking, we return again and again to the movement of our hands. Concentrating with a single focus, either on the rhythm of our breathing or on the rhythm of our knitting, brings us to a sense of relaxation, ease and balance.

In my work as a psychotherapist I run groups for women that I call Knitting as a Spiritual Path—The Wisdom of Craft. In these groups, women learn to use their knitting as a tool for the practice of meditation. The women in these groups seek a deeper, more composed connection to themselves. They come together to find companionship, peace and stillness through knitting. They develop their own spirituality, the expression of their own souls through the work of their hands.

Knitting can be seen as the very process of slowing down and coming home to ourselves—the very thing we have been yearning for in this stressful world. When we can recognize our craft as a profoundly effective meditation practice, we can begin to make conscious use of that daily act of creation as our path to enlightenment. Then, as we fashion our knitted garments, we are also fashioning for ourselves a way of being that is both composed and aware.

A Cloak of Many Colors

Jean Hutchinson

I began knitting in my preteen years with a baby bootie project that I abandoned after one grubby, sadly misshapen, pale yellow bootie of baby wool glared at me, mateless. So ended that knitting phase. Many years later, the yarn bug bit me. I discovered a deep love of color and texture and a fascination with the multitude of patterns. I found I could create patterns of my own. Knitting became my gift to friends and relatives, for Christmas, baby showers, birthdays. I shared my love of color, my time, and my growing skill with those for whom I cared, and they appreciated my gifts. I experimented with machine knitting and learned a whole new range of skills. Sometimes I knit furiously to complete a project or to work out the frustrations of the day. Other times I knit contemplatively, as a peace-filling exercise. Knitting opened conversations, made connections, occupied time with purposeful activity, and resulted in finished and useful products.

I moved away from knitting as a hobby when, for ten years, during a sabbatical from my teaching career, I owned and operated a yarn shop, called Three Bags Full, in Whitehorse, Yukon. I surrounded myself with an array of beautiful (and some not-so-beautiful) yarns, and I spent my time with people who had a similar desire to put their creativity and love of friends and family into gifts of their own talents and enthusiasm. I came to know a diverse knitting community of women and men who expressed themselves and their connection to others through yarns of a different sort, natural and synthetic, knit together through experience, both common and exceptional. For those years, I shifted into a different role—craft teacher, consultant, advisor—always looking for ways to affirm, encourage, connect, help. My own knitting became a matter of making samples and test swatches and giving lessons.

But as often happens when you turn a pleasure into a business, knitting lost its recreational qualities for me. It became a chore, a job, with only the memory of long evenings lost in contemplation. Eventually, I closed my store and returned to teaching. It took a full three-year break from knitting for me to begin to dream about colors and projects and gifts for others again. My first project was to knit and felt mitts for two special friends. My second was to create a vest that depicted Isaiah, Chapter 55, as a project for a course entitled A Hitchhiker's Guide to the Hebrew Scriptures, at St. Stephen's College in Edmonton. But knitting still had not regained the spontaneity, the joy, the contentment it had once held.

With my return to studenthood in the M.A. in St. Stephen's Spirituality and Liturgy program, I began to look for connections between my old interests and my new passion: between the women I'd met at my yarn store and the stories they had shared with me, and theology. The stories made sense and shone with value when I looked at them from a feminist perspective, but they seemed to be more muted in a larger theological purview. Seen by a feminist eye, these women's stories were like a grandmother's gift of a lacy blanket for her beloved grandchild. Viewed through a standard theological lens, however, they looked more like a woman's endless batch of knitted dishcloths made as she rode from Florida to Alaska,

watching the scenery on her husband's "trip of
began to see the relationship between how on
significance of women and their craft and how
is represented in theology and the church. The s
women's spirituality became of great interest to me.

I became fascinated, also, by the layers of meaning in biblical stories, the layers I could now find and the many I knew that still evaded me. I looked for the word "knit" in a concordance and found five occurrences in the New Revised Standard Version. The two in Job implied strength and integrity through knitting, but it was the other three that delighted me. In Chronicles 12:17, the writer said, "If you have come to me in friendship, to help me, then my heart will be knit to you." The psalmist of Psalm 139:13 wrote, "For it was you who formed my inward parts; you knit me together in my mother's womb," and then continued to marvel at the complexity and wonder of such creation. And Paul, in his letter to the Ephesians, said, "But speaking the truth in love, we must grow up in every way into him who is the head, into Christ, from whom the whole body, joined and knit together . . . as each part is working properly, promotes the body's growth in building itself up in love" (Ephesians 4:15–16). These verses seemed to imply a very particular strength in connection and relationship, practiced regularly by women whose value, voice, and significance are often discounted.

I decided to pursue this further and to try to see how women's knitting and women's spirituality might be related. My own experience with knitting could be a starting point. My yarn shop years had taught me the importance of self-investment and the process, as well as the finished product. The hopes expressed by my customers were that the finished knitted garment would fit; that the wearer would like and enjoy it; that it would be a synthesis of skill and knowledge, raw products, and love and become an expression of wholeness and integrity, appreciated for the gift it was; and—always!—that it would have a future, a use, to be worn and admired, to give comfort and pleasure. Knitters invested much more in their projects than a bit of money and time. Their projects were filled with their creators' hopes and dreams and fears.

Now, my passion for making and giving small items like socks and mitts and hats lurks close to the surface, waiting for an opening of time long enough for knitting to become a pleasure again, for long quiet evenings of listening to music and feeling those textured strands flow through my fingers, loop over needles, and become a gift of high quality and pleasure. I often look at the brilliant sunsets or the subtle shades of an autumn mountainside and think of sweaters of soft wool and mohair or crisp cotton, sweaters that speak of things holy, in creation and re-creation. And I think of the pleasure of giving something specially created to a person who will be surprised or delighted to receive a gift of love and time. In the meantime, I admire and appreciate the work of others who find the time to knit.

And the Minister Knit Her Stole

Carole Ann Camp

The balls of purple and pink yarns play on the floor between us. The woman sitting across from me, knitting ferociously, is the new minister of my church. I wondered, when she came, how she would pastor me, how she might give me a glimpse into the female mysteries of my faith, so long buried under the weight of a male-dominated religion. I do not know quite what I expected—and I am sure there are more ideas and experiences yet to come—but my first insight into what her ministry might be like came through an age-old image: women knitting.

During my early women's-liberation years, I hid my yarns and became a closet knitter. After all, what could be more traditionally feminine than knitting and crocheting? I was totally taken off guard, then, when this thoroughly feminist minister mentioned that she was making an altar cloth for Advent and knitting herself a stole. Sewing and knitting were the last things I expected to be confronted with. But the image of a hand-knit minister's stole brought me great excitement, even joy. At first, I wondered at my own response. In time, I realized that my pastor's sewing and knitting freed me to connect again with the ancient arts of women. I could begin to understand myself as a knitter, a weaver, a creator of things.

Since then, knitting and weaving have become a metaphor that helps me enter the mystery and sacredness of life. As I sit and do macramé, for example, I fantasize that the ropes are persons coming together to form an intricate union: sometimes separating, sometimes joining. Some strands never meet. Others are constantly interacting to form patterns of intriguing beauty. Occasionally two or more threads are knotted together out of order. I let them stay, reminding me of the irregularities and surprises in the otherwise orderly routine of my life.

Looking back, I see women in other centuries making fine embroidery and creating delicate patterns of tatted lace, and I know that women were always creating in the ways open to them, when the world of the arts, like painting, was male-oriented. I see women, after hard days in the field or farm or kitchen, sitting (at last!) and sewing a hem. Their sewing legitimized a chance to sit and rest, a chance to claim a piece of time to journey into the inner self. I see women gathered in quilting parties, an early version of today's women's support groups, coming together sharing their lives, their joys and their fears. And in these gatherings, their intimate life stories were quilted into the pattern of the fabric.

I see all of these forms of weaving, knitting, crocheting, macramé, as women's mantras, releasing women from worldly cares to their inner space, a place whose depths provided comfort and strength. And so, this woman minister and I sit and talk. We begin to share our lives. We begin to weave—the pattern unknown, the colors unselected, the textures a secret. Will we create macramé pot hangers in which to plant our seeds of hope? Will we knit mittens or sweaters to clothe the naked? Will we weave blankets to comfort the cold and lonely? Will we embroider a tapestry that records our women's story? Or will we needlepoint cushions on which to kneel and humble ourselves before our God?

A Few Clicks to Spirituality

Dan Odegard

Sitting at dinner with our guests, my wife and I engage in the all-too-infrequent pleasure of genuine adult conversation with friends. The infrequency is the result of an eight-year-old daughter of "geriatric" parents who is confident in herself and well (and loudly) spoken in her demands. While we talk, we hear faint clicks coming from the adjacent family room. "What is Zoë doing?" our friends ask. "Knitting." Silence, and a slight befuddlement follows.

Welcome to the very blessed and wonderful life of the parents of a Waldorf-educated child. It is a principle of Waldorf philosophy, coming from the tradition of Anthroposophy and Rudolf Steiner, that handwork is essential to the spiritual development of the child, regardless of gender or age, from kindergarten on. For the early school child, it's hand-knitting. By second grade, the child is doing European-style knitting, making socks and gnomes and everything that a seven- or eight- or nine-year-old can imagine from those beautiful little knots of cotton and, more frequently, wool. It is tactile, meditative work, enriching both intellect and heart.

And it is, I believe, profoundly spiritual. Not simply meditative, not just a Zen-like trance (or the Western version of it), but truly an accomplishment of union of heart and mind and soul: as good a definition of spirituality as I know. And this observation comes from a witness only. I don't knit. I'm not Rosie Greer (the football star) doing his needlepoint on the airplane between games. Probably the most meditative, repetitive thing I do is to feed the birds and exercise three times a week. Yet I do see this spiritual development in Zoë, in her beautiful sense of things when she knits and purls (a distinction that I admit is still quite mysterious to me) as I read to her before bed or as she talks to a friend on the phone (somehow she manages to make this more a gymnastic accomplishment than a spiritual one, I think).

I sell myself a bit short here, however. I must here gratefully acknowledge my third-grade teacher, Inez Carlson, from Anoka, Minnesota (home of Garrison Keillor and me). If she were teaching in 1995 rather than about 1955 (remember that part about geriatric parents?), she would be a gender-bender, or would be accused of New Age proselytizing. As it was, she just wanted to challenge her charges a bit, and reversed some of the gender roles of the time. For a year, the girls did woodworking and drafting, and the boys did knitting and needlepoint and sewing. No exceptions made, and none were requested, as I recall, a testament to her strength rather than our wisdom. I made embroidered handkerchiefs for my father and an apron for my mother. I learned the basics of knitting at the time, and then promptly forgot them as the more pressing notions of high school shop and cars and girlfriends overtook my one year of enforced wisdom. But knitting stayed with me, I think, and allowed me great comfort, as my son became a decent poet and scholar and my daughter now, at eight, a decent human being. And the handcraft elements of Rudolf Steiner's are, I think, no small part of all of that, whether translated through Inez Carlson in Lincoln Elementary School in 1955, or through Minnesota Waldorf School in 2001.

The clicking then continues in the other room, a pleasant accompaniment to the adult conversation in the dining area of the house. Curiously, Zoë doesn't get frustrated if she drops a stitch or has to pull apart and reknit a piece. She's learning lessons I didn't learn for five decades, and doing so without any obvious effort. One can almost literally witness the pleasure of the handwork come from inside her heart. This is not the arrogant pleasure of a task accomplished, or the pride of effort and result. It is pleasure itself only.

Zoë's teacher may be at times a taskmaster, or so Zoë tells me. But the sense of it all is internal. It is, quite visibly, the union I spoke of earlier of the hand and heart and soul, of the spirituality of creation itself in the activity of the idea, and in the physical representation of the ideal.

Is it just knitting? No, of course not. It's not a metaphor either, or even a pedagogical device. It isn't a trick. And it may not last. Zoë may or may not include knitting and handwork and sewing or whatever as an activity within her daily life. But it will be there, and it will lie in the education of her soul, the early learning of a human being and the effortless discipline of the true heart.

I am as blessed by those clicks nearby as I am by the incense in a church. The bookmark woven by my daughter holds my place in both my book and in my life. We are all bound together, warp and woof, in the intricate web of creation. God's creation, I suppose; but also ours. And it is eternally ongoing. I can hear it in the clicks behind that closed door of both privacy and union.

Tangles

Wren Ross

May she who never got her yarn in a twist throw the first skein. I believe that every knitter alive has spent at least one frustrating moment contemplating a mass of yarn that resembles a year's worth of matted dreadlocks. As a multi-color knitter for over twenty years, I certainly have had my share of them.

Tangles take on a life of their own. I think sometimes that when I leave my knitting in the bag and go to sleep, the yarn starts a mutiny of joining forces and knotting up to make my task impossible the following day. Morning comes, I happily approach my yarn bag, sit down, take out my work, only to confront—the TANGLE. The web, the enemy, the problem. There it is, the representation of all I've done wrong before me. My neglect, my indifference, my bad choices are all represented in this disordered series of knots. How did this happen?

I take it personally. I should have put rubber bands around the skeins, separated them, as the knitting magazine instructed. Why don't I ever listen to advice? I should give my skeins space. I should be more organized. Neater. And then I realize that this tangle has something to teach me about myself: how I get into tangles and (more important) how I get out of them. So I change my attitude and realize this tangle is not a problem. It is an opportunity. This is the first stitch of the "Twelve Stitch Program" toward fiber/emotional health.

Why *don't* I give my yarns space, rubber bands, plastic bags? Maybe for the same reason I don't give myself space for all the different parts of myself. I'm in a rush. I have made a list with so much to do on it that I am going faster than speeding light. Watch a bird outside the window? Take a walk? Meditate? Huh! "Productive Woman" is here and she must work, work, work!!! So when my back is turned, when I'm sleeping or cooking, the yarn, like the neglected parts of myself, gets together and finds a way to make me stop. Take time and disengage from all the extraneous doings to find a quiet way to be.

You must take time to untangle a tangle. It takes focus and observation and lots of patience. There is a Zen lesson in every tangle. It teaches one about really being awake and mindful in the present moment. The Buddhists have that wonderful idea about chopping wood and carrying water. When you chop wood, you chop wood and when you carry water, you carry water. That's all you do. I know I am a chronic multi-tasker and love to see how many activities I can juggle simultaneously. Can I drive, eat, plan a class and talk on the phone at the same time? The result, of course, is tangles.

There are lots of different types of tangles. There are the "quick, get them before they are really bad tangles," with a little knot here or twisted yarn there. Get those early and you are off and running. Just as in a relationship, when you notice a dirty look or cross tone and take the time to smooth it out. "I'm sorry, I didn't mean to talk to you like that." You hug and all is fine. You can continue knitting your lives together harmoniously.

There are more complicated tangles. They happen over

longer periods of time when you ignore what is happening with the yarn. You deny the tangle is happening and so it grows and grows until it looks like an entity in itself. A sculpture symbolizing neglect. Those tangles are challenges. Sometimes they require outside help to get perspective. You also have important choices in these events. You can follow each yarn to see where it goes, undoing it as you go, or sometimes you may decide to cut off as much yarn as you can undo realistically and sacrifice the rest. This raises a question of value. It is harder to sacrifice a rare Angora or silk yarn to a tangle than an acrylic. But then, maybe that acrylic was the last of a special dye lot. Value can be relative.

It is important to be discerning about personal tangles as well. You need to know when to cut yourself off from a toxic individual and when to take on the sometimes laborious task of processing where all the hurts and knots exist in a tangled relationship.

Sometimes tangles are an unavoidable by-product of challenge. If you knit with ten different colors, there's a good chance that you may sometimes find your yarn tangled. It's like running a huge project with lots of different elements—or a family; the odds are in favor of tangles occurring sometime. And by the way, on more than one occasion I have discovered brilliant, offbeat color combinations because they unexpectedly showed up in a big tangle. How many times have you learned something new and important about yourself or a loved one after a fight?

Living a tangle-free life is out of the question. Nature herself creates tangles that are supposed to be intertwined. Think of ivy climbing up a wall or the natural growth patterns of peas or tomatoes. No one would question their beauty or rightness. Tangles can be the result of hyper-involvement. Good or bad, being involved is a way of being alive.

It is important to forgive oneself for one's tangles—yarn or personal. There are always good reasons for them and we are doing the best we can at all times. It certainly doesn't unsnarl a tangle any faster if we are hard on ourselves. Also, tangles are metaphors for confusion; it is said that "confusion is the halfway house to wisdom." The tangle is a flashlight that draws our attention to what needs to be sorted and clarified. The tangle is our teacher, our guide and friend.

The higher part of me knows all this. I know that knitting is an intentional practice of making knots and that often tangles are knots that arise from lack of intention. Lack of mindfulness. I know I am supposed to breathe and be awake, one stitch at a time. That is what I am supposed to do, but I have a confession to make to you. While I have been writing this last paragraph, I have been eating breakfast, undoing a tangle from a wool project from last fall and periodically making phone calls. I guess I am still working on my relationship to tangles.

The Spinner*

Molly Wolf

Now that the end of the school year is in sight (from summer holidays as a working single parent, dear Lord in your mercy, deliver me!), it's field-trip time. On Tuesday my younger son,

John-of-the-bee-brown-eyes, duly trotted off with the rest of Mrs. Caldwell's Grade 4 class for a tour of our local agricultural college. Among other goodies, he brought back a small plastic bag with a fistful of raw sheep's wool.

Way back there in a previous existence, I learned to spin. Never mind why; like so many of my dafter decisions, it seemed like a reasonable idea at the time. So, showing John, I teased the fibers apart, lined them up, and then drew them out, twisting them into yarn.

He was bored out of his mind, of course. After he'd departed in search of better, less psychologically correct amusement (cap guns), I sat down at the kitchen table with the rest of the wool, playing with it and letting my mind wander.

You can clean wool quickly and roughly and efficiently by washing it in detergents that strip the lanolin out and combing it with mechanical carders. Or you can clean wool slowly and gently and inefficiently by teasing the matted fibers apart with your fingertips and letting the dirt fall out. Gently, because tearing at it only rips the fibers and makes for a weaker yarn. The strongest yarn results from thoughtful and careful treatment.

Musing on this and other matters, I played with the wool, teasing it from hand to hand. Some of the roughest, dirtiest bits I laid aside to throw out, but there were batches of soft, almost clean, short-staple underwool, soft as silk, crimped and shining ivory, lovely to the touch. I'd forgotten the feel of this stuff, and what it does to your hands—all that lanolin.

When I finished teasing the wool, the mass was cleaner, much cleaner, but not really *clean*, and I was still in the mood to muse, so I went at it again, loosening the fibers further, letting more dust fall onto the tabletop. I went through the process three times, and when I was done, the wool was a soft, light, airy mass, cream-colored, only slightly flecked with dirt. I put it back in its bag to show John.

I swept up the little pile of dirt—quite innocuous now—and picked up the dirtiest bits of wool, the ones I thought weren't worth trying to clean. Even as I started to throw the filthy wool away, I noticed that it included quite a lot of wool that might, just possibly, be salvageable. These hanks had to be handled a little less gently, but in the end I think I managed to get all the wool out of them and into the bag with the rest. In the end all I threw out was dirt.

If I'd been engaged in real spinning, I would have carded the cleaned wool into rollags with my carding combs. I would have cupped each rollag in my palm, drawing out the fibers between my fingers while the twirling spindle sent the necessary spin creeping up the strand—not too fast!—twisting it into yarn; and then I would let the yarn twirl down onto the spindle. I would have done this with a gentle, rhythmic back-and-forth of the hand, controlling the motion by feel—the whole motion as unconsciously wise and ancient and natural as settling the child on the hip to be carried. And then I would have skeined and washed my yarn and hung it in the sun to dry.

If I were a dyer, I could brew up dyes, from old wisdom and knowledge and what came to hand to color the stuff—indigo for blue, cochineal shells for scarlet, the skins of onions for deep caramel yellow. If I were a weaver, I could stretch my warp and shuttle my weft and pattern my colored yarns into a web. If I were a clever tailor, I could cut and shape and stitch that bright web into garments that a dancer might wear, making creative use of whatever I'd been given to work with. If I were the Dance-maker, I could see this all, from embryo lamb to dancer, and I could pattern the Dance. . . .

When my body fails me and I die, I think I (my soul, that is) will be like that wool after maybe the second or third time I teased it apart with my fingers—still a muddled, confused mass, still full of dust and slightly greasy, anything but white and pure and dryly perfect, but (I hope) not quite so full of sticks and burrs and sheep dung as it was originally. I will be a lot airier and looser and softer than I had been. I hope by then I may have worked most of the knots out.

But I'll still be in need of a whole lot more work, most likely. God alone knows what beauty God—by spinning, dyeing, weaving, cutting, shaping, stitching, creating the dancers, designing the Dance—will make of me after that, in the Life I can only dimly sense but long for with all my heart.

I'll bet God's hands are soft, though. Spinners' hands are soft. Lanolin, all that lanolin.

---

* (Reprinted from *Hiding in Plain Sight: Sabbath Blessings,* The Liturgical Press)

About the Editors and Contributors

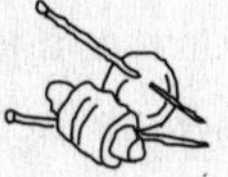

Lisa C. Averyhart was born and raised in Cleveland, Ohio. She began knitting in the fourth grade. Lisa knitted her way through college, where she majored in economics. The needles kept clicking all through Columbia University, where she earned her law degree. Lisa resides in Brooklyn, New York, and practices real estate law when she's not knitting or visiting a yarn shop. She aspires to do more knitwear design and to publish her creations.

Lauren M. Baldwin lives in Albuquerque, New Mexico, with her family—her partner, Vivian, and their children, Ezra (5) and Olivia (2). Besides mothering, Lauren practices law part-time (civil litigation, appeals, adoptions, criminal defense) and tries to squeeze in as much time as possible knitting, writing, and hiking the mountains of the Southwest. Lauren learned to knit at age seven from her mother, Joyce Tarr, and received "advanced training" from the dear women at KnitOne in Colorado Springs, Colorado.

Edward Bear was born in Brooklyn and grew up in Los Angeles. Early adventures included a brief stint in minor league baseball, too many years in construction, day labor, and other dead-end jobs. A correspondence course landed him a job at Hewlett-Packard, where he was employed for nearly thirty years. Previous publications include several fiction pieces in small literary magazines, a baseball novel (*Diamonds Are Trumps*), *The Dark Night of Recovery*, *The Seven Deadly Needs*, and *The Cocktail Cart*. Mr. Bear currently lives in the Rocky Mountains with his wife, plays a vintage Martin guitar, and writes in whatever time the gods and goddesses have left him.

Zoë Blacksin is a passionate knitter, reader, and writer. She started to knit at ten years old, but only seriously threw herself into the craft during high school, when "A Twist in the Yarn" was written as a college application essay. A native of Greenfield, Massachusetts, she now studies and knits at Yale University as an English major, at least until knitting can be classified as a major of study.

Naomi Dagen Bloom, environmental and performance artist, lives on the twenty-first floor of a New York City apartment building, with her husband, Ron, her cat, Lulu, and one thousand busy, composting red worms lowering landfills by eating her garbage. She invites you to join her retirement activity (she was a psychotherapist) and knit a worm. Put on a WormWare™ Party! Bring this Dirt Museum to your town! Visit www.cityworm.com to see how to jump on this twenty-first century worm-wagon.

Janet Blowney has been knitting and collecting yarn since childhood. She belongs to a knit group that meets weekly at a nearby assisted-living community, and lurks in the Knitlist and Socknitters cyber-communities. A year-round supporter of her local yarn shops, in spring and fall she can be found tramping the sheep and wool festivals of New England in search of the perfect fiber. She works as a technical editor to support her yarn habit.

Nan Browning is in her late eighties and still knits whenever she has the chance. She is also an avid gardener and reader of nonfiction and murder mysteries. With her husband she lived and worked in a number of countries in North Africa and the Middle East. When she gets the chance she still travels. She has been to over one hundred countries and always travels with her knitting.

Carole Ann Camp is described as a Renaissance woman. Firstly, she is at ease in the world of science—she has a doctorate in science education and has written several books on women in science. In addition, she is equally comfortable in the world of religion—she is an ordained minister in the United Church of Christ. Carole has coauthored a book on labyrinths and edited books on women's sermons. She also paints, sings, plays the piano, and tap-dances. In her leisure time, she quilts, knits, crochets, embroiders, needlepoints, and sews everything from banners to wedding dresses.

Nancy Chamberlin was born in West Virginia in 1927. As a child, she lived in New Jersey, Maryland, and finally, Delaware. Before earning her B.S. and M.S. degrees from Syracuse University, she was actively involved with the university's theatrical productions. She has also done some summer-stock opera near Plymouth, Massachusetts. She formerly worked with deaf children and infants in Boston, Massachusetts, serving as a Speech and Hearing Therapist in Sussex County, Delaware. Nancy married in 1957, and now has three sons.

Tara Cibelli graduated from Mount Holyoke College in the spring of 2002 with a degree in English and Women's Studies. She plans to pursue a career in publishing in the Boston area. Tara wrote her story for her Memere, who has brought more joy to her life than she will ever know.

Bridget Arthur Clancy is from Wheeling, West Virginia, and currently lives in Philadelphia, Pennsylvania, with her husband, Tim, and their cats, Hannah, Tess, Abigail, and Garden Kitty. She took knitting lessons about five years ago, and enjoys lurking on some knitting-related listservs. Her other interests are animals, history, food, and reading. She works as a reference librarian at the Presbyterian Historical Society in Philadelphia.

Susanna Clarke, an aspiring writer, lives in rural Nova Scotia with her second husband, two teenagers, four cats, and a dog of extremely mixed parentage and strange habits. She knits when the spirit moves her, usually with disastrous results.

Christine Cooper is a member of the Ray of Hope charity knitters in Haslington, England. Since the group of both machine and hand knitters was formed two and a half years ago, it has raised £15,000. Cooper and the group supply Leighton Hospital's neonatal ward with all of their needs in baby blankets, clothing, and crib sheets. The money that they have raised has also gone toward the hospital's purchase of a new MRI scanner. The charity's name, Ray of Hope, was named after borough councilor Ray Stafford, who was mayor of Haslington at the time. You may contact her at chrisrayofhope@yahoo.co.uk or visit the website, www.s-cheshire.ac.uk/babywear.

Frances Lord Corriveau was born in Waterville, Maine. She now resides in western Massachusetts with her long-term partner and their five rabbits. She enjoys singing jazz, hiking the forest trails of New England, and taking long beach walks on the coast of Maine. Her knitting remains marginal but nevertheless enjoyable.

Susan Crawford is a Southern California artist with a great affinity for Southwestern American cultures. She began with a goal of mastering every type of handwork imaginable, and ended up creating in watercolor, mixed media, and monotype. Her awareness has evolved due to her many moves throughout the Southwest, and through her many changes in lifestyle. She still knits, spins, and weaves, but her focus now is on painting. You can contact her at her studio: P.O. Box 655, Cedar Glen, CA 92321

Dalis Davidson started out with two lambs fourteen years ago. She had no idea what to do with all the wool they produced. Fortunately, she knew some wonderful fellow shepherds who taught her to dye, spin, and knit. She started the Dancing Leaf Farm eight years ago, built a studio on her farm, and now provides hand-painted yarn to many customers, taking inspiration for her colors from the surrounding countryside. She is involved with a group of artisans who host three studio tours a year and she also teaches knitting workshops at a local retreat center. She enjoys traveling, mountain biking, kayaking, and she of course takes her knitting wherever she goes.

Valentina Devine grew up in Berlin, Germany, and has always knitted. In fact, she cannot remember who taught her, and she may have even knitted in the womb! She came to the U.S. as a war bride and knitted for her family and friends. Her knitting allowed her to work for a fiber business in New York and eventually start her own business in the eighties. When she moved to New Mexico in the early nineties, she was part owner of a boutique in Santa Fe. She has been teaching "Creative or Abstract Knitting" for eighteen years, throughout the U.S. and in Germany. Valentina dyes her own yarn and is a vendor at different wool and fiber festivals. She now operates out of her own studio, where she designs for different companies and knits one-of-a-kind garments for local boutiques.

Laurie Doran was born and raised in Connecticut. As a teenager, she had designed sweaters for herself under her mother's guidance. She now teaches knitting classes and has sold her knitting at craft and art galleries. Currently, Laurie is writing a novel and pursuing becoming a master climber. She also gives slide presentations on mountaineering. Laurie lives with her husband, Roger, in Maine.

Kay Dorn is a Cape Cod "wash-ashore" from Connecticut—her days are spent canoeing and walking with her husband or volunteering at the library. After many years of writing articles for outdoor magazines, she entered college at forty-eight, and received the award of Truman Scholar from President Truman's daughter, Margaret. Retiring recently from editing a business newspaper, she has extra time to spend knitting, which is even more fun now that she has five grandchildren.

Jay Elliott was born in Los Angeles in 1945. He has taught American literature at Clark University in Worcester, Massachusetts, since 1971, and now lives in Easthampton, Massachusetts. He grew up in Placerville, one of the original gold-mining communities of Northern California, and obtained degrees from Stanford and Indiana Universities. He has a teenage son, whose fascination with sports has rekindled his own enthusiasm, leading him to become an umpire, the activity that dominates his nonacademic summers. He is currently assembling a book of baseball stories.

Elaine Eskesen says her store, Pine Tree Yarns, in Damariscotta, Maine, reflects her flair for the unusual. There she offers spinning classes with hand-dyed roving, a solar dye oven, and a library full of books for her customers. Her philosophy in teaching new and curious knitters has been to listen carefully to her customers, and always keep a good sense of humor. For Elaine, knitting wools and mixing dyes has been an adventurous, yet meditative part of her daily life for almost fifty years.

Hanah Exley was born in the 1920s, which birthed her passion for jazz and singing. She learned to knit in the thirties, and moved to Los Angeles in the forties, where she experienced the effects of World War II. The 1950s brought marriage, children, divorce, remarriage, and more children. The 1970s gave way to her new career as an interior designer, her own art gallery, and her quitting smoking. In the eighties she invented Hanah Silk, and in the 1990s, she spent seven years traveling in China, developing a business called Far Village. The organization was developed with women belonging to a minority group called the Miao. Continuing to develop Hanah Silk made her realize in 2001 that each decade was better than the last!

Rosalia Feinstein was born in England in 1940, and was brought up in Australia from 1948 to 1958, when she moved to Albuquerque, New Mexico. Educated in Albuquerque, Rosalia obtained her bachelor's degree in 1962, and her master of arts in 1968. She has taught French, as well as worked as a child-welfare worker. She has been married since 1960 to a terrific husband, and has two wonderful daughters, two charming sons-in-law, and two marvelous grandchildren. After retiring, she still remains active in Albuquerque, volunteering, learning, reading, attending the theater, taking trips, and making crafts.

Zaina Keller Flickinger was born into a kind and loving family on March 26, 1935, in Middletown, Ohio. Her grandparents played an important part in her upbringing—one grandmother is the subject of her story for *KnitLit*. She graduated from Ohio University in Athens, Ohio, with a major in business education, and taught for thirty years. She married David Jay Flickinger in 1961; she and her husband retired in 1990. She says knitting has always been important to her, because it has enabled her to meet so many talented and interesting people. She belongs to The Knitting Connection of Middletown, Ohio, and serves as vice president and president of the local chapter. She is also a member of the Dayton, Ohio, Knitting Guild and the Education Committee of The Knitting Guild of America.

Lucinda J. Garthwaite doesn't knit, but she does love a good pair of woolen mittens and a warm winter sweater. She earned her masters of fine arts in creative writing at Goddard College, and teaches and writes from her home in Saco, Maine.

Luisa Gelenter's travels in Bolivia allowed her to sit down with Bolivian women and learn how to hand-spin alpaca on a drop spindle. When the time came to dye these handspun yarns, she felt they deserved more than a punch of powder. "The dye was cast," so to speak, and so began her great hand-spinning and plant-dyeing adventures. These experiences formed a clear path of creativity that she now walks down every day.

Jonna Gjevre is an assistant professor of English at the University of Wisconsin, Stout. She enjoys bicycling, bird-watching, cross-country skiing, and (of course) knitting. Her two cats, Cinder and Gabriel, are particularly fond of the deep purple mohair afghan she recently made for them.

Elaine Lang Greenstein is a clinical psychologist in private practice. She has kept her hands busy during conferences and meetings by knitting sweaters for colleagues, friends, family, and their babies. Intricate patterns fascinate her; she analyzes them in her patients' lives and creates them with needles and yarn. She lives in Newton, Massachusetts, with her husband and two daughters, who are the recipients of many creations, with her love knit into every stitch.

Kathryn Gunn lives in Australia. Although her occupation is writing communication boards for use in emergency/aid/refugee settings, her claims to fame are: 1) learning to knit despite having cerebral palsy; 2) bowling out the Australian cricketing legend Sir Donald Bradman at a Crippled Children's Camp "Ashes" match; 3) writing more than 8,000 letters seeking support for what became International Literacy Year because she believes that without the right to a means of communication, there can be no means of upholding the right to freedom of speech.

Christine G. Hagan's curiosity started her knitting at a young age; she was taught by her mother, Peg Genovese. She knitted her way up from doll clothes to sweaters. While she has taught academic writing to high school students for twenty-eight years, this is her first attempt at writing for others. Whether she's at home in Easthampton, Massachusetts, with her husband, Dan, and their son, Dan Jr., or at their summer home in Wellfleet, her knitting needles are always nearby.

Peter Hagerty's Peace Fleece is not your typical yarn company. Its office is a sheep farm in Maine, a crowded family apartment in Moscow, or in the back of a pickup truck somewhere between Tel Aviv and Jericho. Peter Hagerty and Marty Tracy started buying wool from the Soviet Union back in 1985, in hopes that through trade, they could lessen the threat of nuclear war. Since then, they have purchased wool from shepherds in Russia, Romania, Kyrgyzstan, Israel, and the West Bank (as well as Montana, Ohio, Texas, and Maine). By working with people who tend livestock every day, Peace Fleece hopes to find a common ground that can slowly lead to mutual understanding and economic interdependence.

Nancy W. Hall is a developmental psychologist and full-time freelance writer. Born and raised in Tennessee, she is now an accidental Yankee living in an old farmhouse in south central Connecticut with her husband, two kids, two cats, and a dog. In between books and articles about child development, parenting, health, and family policy, she unwinds with karate, kickboxing, bread baking, spinning, and, of course, knitting.

Natalie Harwood was born and raised in the suburbs of Boston. She graduated from Wheaton College, Norton, Massachusetts, with a B.A. in classics. The next forty years consisted of marriage, five babies, graduate school, and teaching at the high school and college levels. She was launched into her writing career as a charter member of the Ohio Writing Project. She has published articles on teaching Latin, short stories, and translations from Latin. Her *Complete Idiot's Guide to Learning Latin* was published in 2000. She is now looking at retirement and time for her eleven grandchildren and numerous knitting projects, which include a bunny-covered onesy that she is developing into a size large enough to fit a kindergartner.

Catherine Hinard is an avid and seasoned knitter. She has long been fascinated by the wisdom of knitting and the spiritual aspects of her own knitting practice. She specialized in transpersonal psychology and spirituality while earning a master's degree in counseling psychology from Lesley College in Cambridge, Massachusetts. She was also a resident and staff member for seven years at the Kripalu Yoga Center in Lenox, Massachusetts. Catherine has over twenty years of experience working with textiles, weaving, and knitting, and has created groups for women called Knitting as a Spiritual Path, The Wisdom of Craft. She is currently working at Webs Yarn Store in Northampton, Massachusetts. Catherine welcomes discussion on this article. You can e-mail her at chinard@yahoo.com

Jennifer Hope, native Hoosier and Indiana University graduate, is wife to John, mom to John William, and employed full-time as a Web developer. Her love of knitting began at age six and she has knit everything from pillows to gloves, sweaters, and clogs. She prefers to hand-knit Aran sweaters and socks and likes to machine-knit quick projects for family and friends. She is spreading the love of knitting by teaching children and adults in her Fort Wayne, Indiana, community. She hopes to expand her teaching career by becoming a certified instructor and teaching workshops nationwide. Her other hobbies include scrapbooking, photography, golf, and sewing.

Jean Hutchinson is Jennifer's mum, a theology student, and a lover of color and texture. In past lives, she has been an adult basic education instructor in Whitehorse, Yukon, a yarn shop owner in Whitehorse, and a physical education teacher in Edmonton, Alberta. When her studies are over, she plans to spend long, dark evenings sitting in an easy chair, listening to mellow jazz, sipping tea, and knitting socks of the most outrageous and extravagant colors.

Mary Keenan is a Toronto-based freelance writer with a weakness for all things construction-related, from clothing to dollhouses to home renovation. When not busy making something or hunting for collectibles of 1920s–50s vintage, she writes comic mysteries. You can visit Mary's website at www.marykeenan.com, or e-mail her at mary@marykeenan.com.

Harry Kelley spins and knits at True North Farm in Earlton, New York, an Icelandic sheep dairy where he also milks one hundred Icelandic sheep. He has worked as a vice president for Young and Rubicam Advertising and as a chaplain at Bard College in Annandale-on-Hudson, New York. He grew up in West Virginia, and was taught to knit by his grandmother, Georgia Ellen, and her sisters, Ona Mae, Lona Fae, Melly Maude, and Flota Olive.

Pam Kohan is described by her friends as always attached to a ball of yarn. A highly visible knitter, she has been knitting for over twenty years, and enjoys teaching at Marji's Yarn Crafts in Granby, Connecticut. She is a permanent fixture in the stands of her three sons' many baseball games, knitting in hand. Her husband, Jim, occasionally wonders aloud, "Wouldn't you like to put that down for a minute and relax?" "NO!"

Elliott Kronenfeld knits every day. Living in Brookline, Massachusetts, with his partner, Tony, he relishes all the projects he has piled around the house. When asked how he can create amazing finished products, he responds, "It's like everything else—it's easy when you know how!" His retirement dream is to own a yarn store with an ocean view. In the meantime, he can be seen knitting in airports around the world!

Marisa Labozzetta is the author of the novel *Stay with Me, Lella* (Guernica Editions, 1999). Her short stories have appeared in such literary magazines as *The American Voice*, *The Florida Review*, and *Via*. Marisa's work has also been anthologized in the bestselling *When I Am an Old Woman I Shall Wear Purple* (Papier-Mache Press), *Show Me a Hero* (Persea Press), *Paradise* (Florida Literary Foundation Press), *Our Mothers, Ourselves* (Greenwood Press), and of *Italian American Writers*, ed. Regina Barreca (Penguin Books). She lives in Northampton, Massachusetts.

Miriam Lang's first knitting project was a ghastly pair of baby blue slippers produced at the age of nine under the tutelage of her mother. Since then she's created countless more attractive articles of clothing for her family and friends. Miriam is also accomplished at crewel work and embroidery, in which medium she created a freehand representation of her childhood home. Also known as Miriam Lang Budin, she is a librarian in Chappaqua and lives with her husband and sons in Hastings-on-Hudson, New York.

Caroline Laudig was practically born with a needle and thread in hand. At five she sewed her first dress and learned to knit when she was seven. She has rarely been without a needle since. Her friends assume that if she's not knitting, it's time to check her temperature! Her passion is lace knitting, mostly shawls, and she collects stitch dictionaries in all languages. Caroline lives in Indiana.

Susan Lydon is the author of two books: *The Knitting Sutra: Craft as a Spiritual Practice* and *Take the Long Way Home: Memoirs of a Survivor.* She edits and teaches, has contributed articles and reviews to many national publications, and writes a regular newspaper column when she can tear herself away from her knitting. She lives in Northern California. An earlier version of this article appeared in *Interweave Knits*.

E. Anne Mazzotta was born in Newfoundland in the early fifties. Life was full of family, friends, and lots of fun in the great outdoors. Her mother and father continued to run the corner store and sell fishing supplies while their six children were growing up. After dating for three years, she and her new husband moved to his home in New York City, and later to Canton, New York. While raising three sons and a daughter, Anne received a B.A. and M.A. from St. Lawrence University. After her children started school, she spent eight years as a nutrition coordinator with St. Lawrence County Head Start. Presently, she is poised to begin a new career as a writer. She continues to enjoy knitting, but declares that she will never be as skillful as her mother, who at the age of eighty-five continues to knit to the great delight of her family.

Karen McCullough learned the basics of knitting when she was ten years old. She was fortunate enough to have an aunt who was a professional knitter to teach her some of the finer points of knitting when she was a teenager. Attending nursing school interrupted her knitting and, unfortunately, working for a living interrupts it now. She has very little spare time so she mostly knits hats for Caps for Kids or the Santa Train for the underprivileged in Walkersville, Maryland (where her husband, the frustrated train engineer, volunteers).

Sallie McFague is the Distinguished Theologian in Residence at the Vancouver School of Theology in British Columbia, Canada. She taught for thirty years at Vanderbilt University Divinity School in Nashville, Tennessee, where her children and grandchildren still live. She writes books in the areas of ecology, Christianity, and economics, her most recent being *Life Abundant: Rethinking Theology and Economy for a Planet in Peril* (Fortress Press, 2000).

Anne McKee was raised on the Canadian prairies. After finishing high school in Swift Current, she headed for the bright lights of the University of Saskatchewan. She decided geology was her thing, and spent the next six years alternating summers in the bush with winters at the desk. Her mineralogy professor at the University of Waterloo suggested, after reading her geofantasy essays, that she should consider becoming a science writer. After realizing that there is as much mystery in crime as there is in science, she decided to write mysteries. She lives in the cedar swamps of eastern Ontario with a laptop, a husband, three children, and a corgi.

Betty Meakim was born and raised in Amherst, Massachusetts. In 1988 she moved two miles away to Hadley, but still keeps contacts with family and friends in Amherst. After graduation from Amherst High School, she attended commercial college. In 1937 she began working at Amherst College and retired in 1982. Her work was in several offices, but the most gratifying was meeting and helping students. Along the way she raised four children, and her knitting has been an ongoing project.

Scott Morris is a family practice physician and ordained United Methodist minister who founded the Church Health Center in 1987. The Center provides quality medical care for those in need—and does it with a broad base of support from the faith community as well as volunteer physicians, nurses, optometrists, and dentists. By uniting churches and synagogues with health care professionals and the community, the Church Health Center cares for more than thirty thousand patients, without any government assistance.

Janet Muench was born in Elkhart, Indiana, into a family steeped in Swedish tradition. She learned to knit and play the piano as a child. Over the years, she has tried out many other crafts and musical instruments, but knitting and piano have won out as her true passions. Her husband of forty-three years and their two grown sons do not wear wool sweaters, but socks, mittens, and scarves fulfill her desire to make things for the men in her life. As a member of the Communications Department at National Church Residences, a nonprofit housing provider for low-income families, she became more involved in graphic design, a skill that carries over into her knitting now.

Elena Latham Murphy's early life was spent in Easton, Maryland, where waterfowl abound and the blue crab is king. She was always a hands-on person, enjoying crafts such as crocheting, needlepoint, counted cross-stitch, crewel embroidery, smocking, and the closest to her heart, and also her sanity saver: knitting! She has been married for seventeen years and is a mother to two beautiful girls, ages thirteen and sixteen. Her garments are mainly made for children, as they work up quickly.

Lucy Neatby is a passionate knitter who designs and writes knitting patterns to entertain the mind as well as the fingers. She shares her love and knowledge of the art by giving a myriad of entertaining workshops. Colors, textures, and arcane techniques enthrall her, as she particularly loves working on tiny needles to achieve the finest quality of work; for her, time is not a consideration! She has dabbled in spinning, bobbin lace, and felting, but her first love will always be knitting. Lucy Neatby, Tradewind Knitwear Designs, kits, patterns, and cool tools for knitters! www.tradewindknits.com, 45 Dorothea Dr., Dartmouth, NS B2W5X4, Canada. Toll free: (866) 272-7996 or (902) 434-5179; fax: (902) 434-0345. Visa now accepted. E-mail: info@tradewindknits.com. Annabelle's Caps—a collection of (approximately twenty and counting!) hat patterns, many from well-known designers—is now available from Lucy. All proceeds go to cancer charities. Please inquire!

Dan Odegard has had a checkered career throughout his life, moving from academic life (as a political theorist) and the military into the book business as a bookseller, literary agent, consultant, editor, publisher, and as the presenter of a series of books based upon a work entitled *A Course of Love*, published in 2001 by New World Library. He treats knitting as a spectator sport, especially through his involvement in Waldorf education as a parent and volunteer. He lives in Saint Paul and is father to Zoë, the knitter, and is husband to Wilma and father to Peter, student-knitters.

Shulamith Oppenheim is an author of books and short stories for children. In her junior year at Radcliffe College, she met and married Felix Oppenheim, a Belgian professor of political philosophy—with Albert Einstein, a longtime friend of the family, as best man. After her first grandchild, Noah, was born, she started the tradition of writing books for each grandchild, featuring them as the hero. Sophie, adopted from China, will soon have hers. Her latest books are a collection of mermen tales, entitled *The Fish Prince and Other Stories*, and *Ali and the Magic Stew*.

Erica Orloff is a writer living in southern Florida. She is the author of several books, which she writes in her "free time" after running around caring for three kids and a house full of unruly pets. She is from a long line of knitters, but the "knitting gene" apparently skipped her. She thinks about her Grandma Irene every day. . . .

Kirsten Ossorio heads a social science research institute at Boston University, and lives with her partner and two cats in Arlington, Massachusetts. Her regular activities include swimming and metalworking. She has written several books, two of them literary nonfiction, and is working on a new novel. Every Saturday and Sunday evening, you will find her knitting at an A.A. meeting. (The name she uses for her literary publications is a pseudonym, in accordance with the Alcoholics Anonymous tradition of maintaining public anonymity.)

Jennifer Parko has been knitting since 1997. Currently she lives, crafts, and occasionally smokes in San Fransisco.

Nicole Pritikin has been knitting for over ten years. In order to support her knitting habit, she has had to drive long distances over the treacherous mountains of Vermont to the nearest yarn store, only to find them out of what she needed. So, to provide an easy way for all knitters to buy quality yarn, she opened an online yarn shop, The Naked Sheep, www.nakedsheep.com, in January of 2000. In May of 2001, the business expanded, opening a retail shop in Bennington, Vermont.

Linda Quigley has been a newspaper writer and editor since 1970 and is coauthor of *Speak the Language of Healing: Living with Breast Cancer Without Going to War*. She grew up in north Alabama, where she was more adept at baiting a fish hook than at keeping stitches equally taut when transferring them from one knitting needle to another. Now living in Nashville, she neither fishes nor knits, but has interesting memories of both.

Linda Roghaar is a native New Englander. Born and raised in Massachusetts, she also has deep connections (yarn and otherwise) to Maine, New Hampshire, and Vermont. Linda has a bachelor's degree in religion from Miami University (Ohio) and a master's degree in liberal studies from Vanderbilt University. The mother of two daughters, she has worked in publishing for almost thirty years and is a literary agent in Amherst, Massachusetts.

Wren Ross is a professional actor, singer, and, above all—truly devoted knitter. She loves working with colors and creates coats that tell personal stories, which she calls Soul Sweaters. Wren also sings a program of Yarn Songs for the Taos Wool Festival in New Mexico. She has designed for Classic Elite, Rio Grande Wools, and Lalana Wools. Wren has been acting for twenty years, and has spent ten years performing in *Shear Madness*. She has also done voice-overs for television, documentaries, and museums. Wren has worked with Jason Robards, Walter Cronkite, Mason Adams, and Cher.

Christine Rusch is a playwright who lives and works in South Carolina. Her plays have appeared on stages in the U.S. and abroad. Her story "Grandmothers Are Supposed to Sit and Knit" is adapted from her comedy *Lemonade Lagoon*.

Kim Brody Salazar is a senior proposal manager who specializes in answering high-tech and engineering-procurement requests. When not consumed by deadlines, she enjoys relaxing with stitching and knitting. She has maintained a knitting-oriented website since 1995. She and her husband, Fernando, have developed that early site into www.wiseneedle.com. On it Kim offers free knitting patterns, and a database of yarn information, including an extensive library of consumer-generated yarn reviews. Kim, Fernando, and their two daughters currently live outside Boston, Massachusetts.

Donna Schaper is the senior pastor at the Coral Gables Congregational Church in Coral Gables, Florida. A prolific author, speaker, and commentator, she says her life goal is to provide spiritual nurture for public capacity. Her voice is often heard on National Public Radio.

Joanne Seiff, educator, writer, hand-spinner, and hand-knitter, lives with her husband and dog in Durham, North Carolina. She has academic degrees from Cornell University, George Washington University, and the University of North Carolina at Chapel Hill, but enjoys most the tactile self-discovery of the world around her. Reveling in the process of creation from scratch, Seiff loves to cook, garden, make preserves, make music, and integrate women's skills from times past into the twenty-first century.

Jennifer Colyer Smith is a young Navy wife and the mother of two girls. She spent most of her youth raising merino sheep on a vintage farm in New England. She learned to knit at her mother's side as a young girl and today she designs children's sweaters for her mother's merino wool shop. Jennifer's Aunt Sally was a personal inspiration in many aspects of her life, including knitting. "Never Say Die" is a tribute to Sally.

Jean Stone is a bestselling author of nine novels (women's fiction) from Bantam Books. Her latest, *Trust Fund Babies*, is a delicious romp with three women who had it all—sex, wealth, and status—then suddenly learn their money is gone and their old secrets no longer protected. A former advertising copywriter and native New Englander, Jean has incorporated Martha's Vineyard into several of her books. She graduated from Skidmore College, in Saratoga Springs, New York.

Connie Elizabeth Tintinalli was born in Windsor, Ontario. She studied fine art at the Ontario College of Art and Design and earned a bachelor of architecture degree from the University of Waterloo. After living in Toronto for seventeen years working mainly in the field of architecture—with forays into modeling, acting, and illustrating—she has recently escaped to the beautiful town of Niagara-on-the-Lake, Ontario, where she hopes to make things—stories, paintings, gardens, sweaters. . . .

Luis Tovar is a single man, aspiring novelist, and freelance editor. He resides in Albuquerque, New Mexico, where he enjoys the desert outdoors, taking long hikes in the coolness of the mornings, identifying pot shards, collecting arrowheads, and meditating on life's lessons. On occasion he returns to his watercolors and has a coffeehouse show where his works are displayed. An avid chess player of mediocre strength, he occasionally plays a rated game or two.

Faye Whyte started knitting at age five. Her first effort produced a trapezoid with a hole in the middle. Her first literary endeavor was her third-grade Christmas play. Now a wife and mother, she continues to knit for family and friends. Her interest in writing has recently been renewed and she is working on two nonfiction projects and a novel. Both pastimes provide welcome relief from her demanding work as a veterinarian. You may contact her at: fwhyte@kingston.jkl.net.

Margaret Klein Wilson is the owner of MOSTLY MERINO, a fiber studio specializing in hand-dyed luxury yarns and custom knit sweaters and knitting kits. A shepherd, dyer, and designer, she credits a rural Wisconsin childhood for her abiding respect for the connection between all things, and her lifelong fascination for process in all matters. She writes and keeps sheep in Dummerston, Vermont.

Molly Wolf, who lives down the street from Anne McKee, shares a shabby white Victorian house with her husband, her two teenage sons, and four cats. Her three collections of kitchen-table theology include *Hiding in Plain Sight* (Catholic Press Association's Best First Book, 1998), *A Place Like Any Other*, and *Angels and Dragons: On Sorrow, God, and Healing*. Her fourth book, *Child on My Father's Arm: Sabbath Blessings*, is in the process of being published. To sample her work, go to: justus.anglican.org/sabbath-blessings.

Jackie Young, teacher and designer, currently manages a retail yarn shop in Fort Wayne, Indiana. She learned to knit from a neighbor at the age of eight. In her high school years she would often make up her own designs, since she did not know knitting patterns even existed! On a family vacation to Maine, Jackie discovered some old copies of Elizabeth Zimmermann's newsletters and immediately wrote to her to learn more about her Knitting Camps. Jackie credits her strong sense of design with the lessons she learned from these early experiences.

Kathy Zimmerman is an accomplished knitter, teacher, and knitwear designer who owns a yarn shop in western Pennsylvania called Kathy's Kreations. Many of her designs feature textures, cables, and novelty ribs, earning her the nickname "Cable Queen" at her local knitting guild. Kathy is the president of Laurel Highlands Knitting Guild in Ligonier, Pennsylvania. You may visit her website at www.kathyskreations.com.